ANY LESS YOU

ANY LESS YOU

A FAMILY HISTORY

Douglas W. Milliken

Fomite
Burlington, VT

ISBN-13: 978-1-959984-24-5
Library of Congress Control Number: 2024931745

Fomite
58 Peru Street
Burlington, VT 05401
www.fomitepress.com

02-04-2025

For my siblings,
the ones I hold and the ones I've lost,
similarly sprung from yet discretely
berthed in this soil we may yet
call home.

Contents

I

(EVIDENCE)

But everything is forgotten, nearly everything,
and sooner rather than later, please God—
fathers, friends, they pass
into your life and out again, a few women stay
a while, then go, and the fields
turn their backs, disappear in rain.

—Raymond Carver, "Prosser"

fig. 1: a southward view from the northern property line, 3x3 print on 126 square format film, 1973.

A line divides the setting. Faintly purple and faintly grey, a washed-out sky dominates the upper two-thirds, gauzed in the thinnest quilt of clouds. Below, a two-acre hash of tall, golden grass Xs and bends in the wind off New Brunswick's breast. And where these two color fields collide, a line divides the setting. This line is where our farm exists. Reading the line from left to right, east to west: the dark steeple of a spruce, the rough pyramid of a maple, the weathered-grey gable-end of the house—two windows above, two windows below—the connected ell and barn, and set a little ways off, the remains of a collapsed outbuilding almost but not quite reaching the midpoint of the line. Past the outbuilding: an indistinct horizon ending in a copse of poplars quaking at the picture's western edge.

On the photograph's reverse, my mother's faded script: **this is the farm we're buying.**

The farm. My mother's home for thirty-five years. More than half her life. Two divorces and four children and innumerable animals and arguments and summer barbecue dinners shared under the

front yard maple. Her adulthood spent on a Northern Maine farm atop a blustery hill. The last
house on a dead-end road. A place for hope and hope deferred.

This is the farm we're buying.

I WANT TO SAY IT PRETTY but fuck it, here's the truth: my entire life as a writer has been a struggle to find a safe way to talk about home. The home I miss and long for. The home I never had. And as much as I long to convince myself otherwise, this struggle isn't yet ended. I know my first book, *White Horses*, certainly feels like home, although the feeling's based completely on abstraction, as nearly nothing concrete about my upbringing—the house where I lived, the members of my family—exists anywhere in that text. But still, it's home. My guess is that writing *White Horses* felt safer than the actual life I was living at the time. It contains a world to which I retreated when I felt I had nowhere else to go. Even though it was ugly there. Even though everything hurt.

For better or worse, the book you are holding feels like home as well.

fig. 2 & 3: my sister and me, 3x5 print on 110 film, May 1983.

Winter-brown patches showing through new grass in the field behind the house. In figure 2, a nearly colorless eastern sky above a backdrop of poplars and spruce clustered across the unpaved road, a couple of leafless red-twig dogwood blazing off the soft shoulder. [Not pictured: the green scent of spring-stunned grass, the tart whiff of nearby animal pasture, the lingering bite of winter on the breeze.] Nearly centered in the frame, my sister Tanya sits in the grass with her knees drawn up to her chest. Beat tennis shoes, navy shorts, white T-shirt, enormous glasses. Her left hand is raised in a visor across her forehead to shield her eyes from the sun. Her other arm forms a casual geometry: right elbow on right knee, right wrist through the crook of her left elbow, right hand relaxed in a droop. She's skinny, maybe because she's thirteen or maybe because we're poor. Or both. Dark curls tumble down her lean shoulders. The look on her face—the shape of her mouth—is disbelief verging on disgust. She is looking directly at the camera.

Before her, on my hands and knees, I clamber through the grass. Blue overalls. Red and white striped T. Blonde hair parted on the left. Brow furrowed against the sun and bottom lip in a milk-fed pout. Weeks away from my first birthday.

The second picture is likely taken moments later, vantage shifted to the northwest: the photographer has circled my sister and me. Tanya is crouching now, one knee in the grass, and we are holding one another. I am clutching her, face buried against her right shoulder, and her arms cup my body in an obvious gesture of comfort, of consoling. Her face is mostly obscured by her hair, but unmistakable is the concern in her eyes, in the shape of her brow.

I have no doubt that my father took these pictures. The evident discomfort in my sister being observed. The narrative implied by the two photos side by side. My father is who took these pictures.

In the background of figure 3: a white and black cow approaches.

OURS WAS A RETIRED horse farm at the top of a windswept hill deep in the dairy- and potato-country of Aroostook County, that big northern panhandled chunk of Maine that, until 1842, was part of colonial New Brunswick. If you can imagine a scaled-down version of the western prairielands of Wyoming racing up toward the Bighorns' cleft toes, then you've got a pretty good idea of what our view was like. Long rolling hills painted in the near-black of evergreens, the bone-white of poplars, the tawny blonde of grassy fields. The far-off ghosts of the Appalachians bluely haunting the horizon. Maybe only half a dozen farmhouses scattered in the distance between.

Mum bought the farm in the early 1970s with her first husband, Tom. They'd fled from Syracuse, New York to this isolated edge of America (if you crossed the road away from the house, no joke, you would literally be standing in the first grasping scrub of New Brunswick) to stake their homestead as part of the Back-to-the-Land Movement. A few of their friends had preceded them up there, but nearly none of them lasted to see the decade through. The country in Aroostook is brutal, the winters obscenely harsh, the locals not always excessively welcoming to these strangest kind of strangers (seriously, what's the farmer's son of a farmer's son supposed to make of a freaky white guy in a dashiki, reeking of hash and pontificating on chakras and vibrations?). Few are the people who are made for that remote northern world. It's a landscape of loneliness. It's rarefying. But Mum loved it up there. With its fanged wind and wide-open personless-ness, it was the first place in all her life where she actually felt at home.

Together, Tom and Mum were able to resuscitate the old farm, which had been left abandoned for nearly a generation. Birds in the rafters and skunks in the outhouse. Surrounded by pasture and woodlot, blackberry patches and feral apple orchards. They raised two children—my sister, Tanya, and my brother, Jaison—before eventually getting divorced. With Bill, my father, Mum later had two more children, my older brother, Daniel, who died at birth, and a year and a half later, me. My father had a child from a previous relationship, too, but we were not raised together and have in essence remained strangers our entire lives. Much later—after Mum's second divorce, during the protracted suit for full-custody of me—the man who would become Mum's third husband entered the picture. He had two children from a previous marriage as well, but again, they were not consistently a part of our family life.

I take the time to detail this list—the members of my immediate family—mostly to illustrate a point. All of these people passed in and (more than anything) out of the world I considered home. In a physical sense, they were anything but constant. But something of their presence—and, more importantly, their absence—was always there, like an emotional thumb-print. Or maybe a better metaphor is the tree in one of our back pastures that, sometime in the prehistory before we lived there, someone—lacking a fencepost—had wrapped a length of wire around. The fence was long gone, but the wire was still there, embedded in the bark. The tree, through the years, had grown to swallow it whole. In this way, our home was never rid of its ghosts. There was always something missing—be it a person or an idea or just a reason why—some shadow dimly flickering just beyond the edge of anything you could possibly see.

fig. 4: Jaison and Bill in the driveway, 3x5 print on 110 film, March 1982.

One of the few photographs I have of my father. Half-turned toward the camera in a brown flannel shirt, dark blue work jeans. Sunglasses. Bushy beard. Wind-blown hair. The photograph is almost completely white with snow, drifting to swallow a snowmobile and a tractor parked at the driveway's edge, the orchard of denuded apple trees, the leaning chicken house. Through all his hair, it is impossible to read Bill's expression.

The same cannot be said for my brother. Dressed in a dark snowsuit, orange and blue mittens and a matching knit cap, Jaison is beaming, his mouth opened wide with laughter. He's smiling so hard his eyes are all but shut. He is standing near the fender of a snow-swept Dodge Pinto. He is waving at the camera. Whatever is happening this winter morning, it is clearly enough to render Jaison insane with joy.

This might very well be the strangest piece of evidence amid what scant documentation I have of my family: my brother expressing any measure of happiness in the presence of my father.

Seeing this picture, every time, I cannot help feeling sad. I never had a chance to know my brother when he was still a laughing Buddha. I wish I could have been alive when that blissed-out child, hysterical with delight, still inhabited my brother's body and brain.

Meanwhile:

My father's slight stoop.

His unkempt ruffle of hair.

The beard engulfing his face.

This so easily could be me as an adult, unmoored from time and standing with my six-year-old brother in the snow two arctic months before I was born.

ABSENCES. MY SISTER, TANYA, being twelve years older than me, moved out and was on her own by the time I was four. Jaison, seven years older, spent as much time away from home as possible until he too was old enough to leave (although it is worth noting that he included me in his escapes as often as he could, taking me camping or fishing or cross-country skiing with his friends all through high school, later putting me up during my school vacations to work with him as the worst imaginable concrete mason, to see touring metal bands and mosh with strangers, to eat mushrooms and funnel beers in different fields, in different woods, to give me a chance to experience something other than the constricting alienation of home). Daniel I never could know, but the idea of him was always around (an idea made tangible by the blue box of ashes tucked beneath my mother's bed, by the Japanese tree lilac that I one day would plant in the yard by Mum's greenhouse, his silvery ashes sown among its roots, among the ripe soil of our farm, among the tree's most beautiful name: *syringa reticulata*). My paternal grandmother, Barbara, lived only two hours south of us, but the rest of my extended family—my other grandparents, my aunts and uncles and cousins—were at best hundreds but mostly thousands of miles away, in New York or Florida or California, virtually unknowable. There was a greater sort of distance between me and my stepfamily. When my father lost his bid for full-custody, he evacuated himself almost completely from my life: from ages nine to seventeen, I did not once see Bill and only very rarely heard from him. I'm sure he had his reasons. I'd be in my twenties before we had anything approximating a relationship.

Mum, of course, was always there. She hated leaving the farm. But she found other ways of being absent. Distracted or unhearing or, most alarming, staring you down like a warding watchdog, like you were a stranger intruding in her house. I'm sure she had her reasons, too.

These sorts of absences create a palpable silence: you can think up all the questions you like, just don't speak any aloud. It makes for a narrative full of holes. In fiction, this would be an excellent context for a mystery. But this is how I grew up. It instilled a fundamental lack of understanding as to who I was, of my present and my past. A numbing buffer between me and the rest of the world.

fig. 5-7: three sunsets, 1973, 1977, 1999.

Three photographs sharing the same composition. Same contours of westerns hills. Same sun exploding behind the horizon. Same angle. Same aim. The first photograph (a 3x3 inch print on 126 square format film) is summer or early-fall—the soft shape of the skyline betrays leaves still clinging lushly to the trees—the landscape almost entirely black as the sun sinks behind the collapsed outbuilding and somnolent distant hills, liquid yellow gradating upward into smoky bluish-grey. All but the roofline of the chicken house is lost in the black below. A faint suggestion of bushes. The barest indication of an apple tree. There's a warmth to all this darkness.

The second picture—also 126 square format—is winter and only slightly less engulfed in black. You can make out the slope of lawn, the ragged thatch of the berry patch, the slump of the chicken house, the stretching fields across faraway hills. Instead of yellow, the sun and sky flare through shades of pink. The collapsed outbuilding is gone. What isn't lost in shadow is drifted in pink-tinted snow.

The third photograph—a 4x6 print from a disposable 35mm point-and-shoot camera—again, is winter. Instead of pink, the world is glossed in the coldest blue, the sun a decreasing yellow cinder behind the hills. What isn't lost in shadow is locked in a fist of blue ice.

All three pictures were taken from the exact same spot, at the end of the driveway, above the wooden platform covering the old well (a well that'd long run dry and whose cover was brittle with rot, a known danger we did nothing about, never replaced, rebuilt, shored up: a threat ever-present right outside our door). All three photos contain the same hills, the same trees, the same increasingly haggard chicken house. The same landmarks and monuments that defined our lives on the hill. Figures 5 and 6, I suspect, were taken by my mother. The first in the verdant months after she and her first husband bought the farm. The second in the final months of their marriage, before the divorce and the introduction of my father into this lonesome tree-lined world. The third photograph, I captured, in my final winter before leaving home. Yet it'd be nearly ten years before I discovered this synchronicity, my mother and I hypnotized through decades by the same indelible western skyline, the same indelible flash of light lost behind the world's curve, the stark reality of where we stood versus the abounding unknown beyond the edge of what little we could see.

Given the nature of sunsets and the mechanics of photography, my mother and I were each likely trying to capture something that was already gone.

OUR HOUSE ON THE HILL.

Its board-and-batten siding weathered grey from unquantifiable blizzards, thunderstorms, summer hail, autumn sleet.

Its fieldstone foundation.

Its three separate chimneys, indicating at a glance how bitterly cold our hilltop could become.

The house's front door—oddly elaborate, scrolled and stained hardwood with a brass knob and an enormous glass oval dominating its center—facing east toward the parallel lines of our dirt road and the inconceivably proximate border, just a single line of wire strung between lank metal stakes mostly hidden among the brambles with the ranks of spruce beyond waving greetings from the New Brunswick fringe.

Through the front door, a set of foot-worn stairs led from the entryway to the bedrooms above. (The bottom step was in fact a trapdoor, concealing a secret compartment where Mum kept her photographs and, for many years, her freshest harvest of weed). To the right—the north—was a room that for most of my life was the living room but in later years became my mother's bedroom. To the left was the combined kitchen/dining area: exposed post and beam oiled a deep red, the floor's unfinished plywood painted chocolate brown, the wallpaper pale yellow (or anyway, yellowed) flowers and teapots in ascending miniature ranks, two sets of south-facing bay windows—one on either side of the woodstove—oftentimes with an enormous kola bud of marijuana tacked to dry from the pane. And on every free surface, houseplants rising and overflowing from pots. Angel-wing begonias. Hindu rope plants and pits-of-snakes. All the cabinetry, Mum's first husband built from wood gleaned from a collapsed outbuilding: on the inside panel of one cabinet door ran a penciled diary from earlier in the century, single-line dated entries concerned mostly with the comings and goings of a perennially loose cow.

What else about the kitchen? There were two wooden barrels, maybe five gallons each, containing flour or rice or, for a period or five or six years, all my plastic Smurf figurines. There was a door painted black that led to the cellar stairs. There was a vertical line of three enormous Artist's Conk mushrooms, shellacked and mounted on the western wall as shelves for Mum's teapots, and always to the right of those mushrooms hung a framed print on loan from the town library—for the longest time a years-overdue reproduction of Andrew Wyeth's *Christina's World*—to cover a hole my father had shot through the wall.

Andrew Wyeth's *Christina's World* is another good point of reference. The house and land in that painting look an awful lot like how our house existed up until the late 1980s.

It is also worth noting how often my mother would tell me:

The woman in that picture is crippled.

The woman in that picture is me.

All the time. From the moment my parents separated until the suit for custody ended. All the time, Mum would point at Christina lying stranded in the grass, the distant farmhouse both something to crawl toward and crawl from, a refuge and a threat.

The woman in that picture is crippled.

She had to count and roll all her change to pay the painting's overdue fine.

The woman in that picture is me.

My father had once tried to a shoot a weasel running loose throughout the house. That's why there's a hole in the wall: he missed.

The four bedrooms upstairs were small and rarely occupied by any one of us for more than a couple years. (For whatever reason, we each of us enjoyed or at least got used to an occasional rearranging of space.) The southern bedrooms looked out over the driveway and garden, then a long meadow of tall grass and wildflowers edged by our nearest, best line of apple trees, then our seventy acres of evergreen woodlot, and beyond that—as the topography declined continually toward the coast almost one hundred miles away—the hazy suggestions of the nearest Grand Lakes. The northern bedroom windows looked out over a two-acre field (sometimes potatoes, sometimes wheat, sometimes fallow with clover, and most years tended by a farmer down the road), then our nearest neighbor's dilapidated shanty, and faintly past that, the red brick of the retired custom-house half a mile away, then little more than uninterrupted sky.

These are the things that are certain. Everything else about the house was in flux. When I was very young, there was an ell and porch off the back of the kitchen—a rugged space dominated by enormous skeletal barn spiders and their gauzy graveyard webs—then a tall barn with a hayloft where our fowl preferred to roost above the threshing floor. As far as I know, these were part of the original farm built sometime around 1860. But eventually, these structures were torn down and replaced with newer additions: a bigger living room extending off the kitchen and an attached, open greenhouse. Meanwhile, our long front yard was replaced by a shoddy attempt at a two-car garage and a makeshift breezeway whose fly-specked bay-window was always fogged from a bad seal. No more view of Canada through our ornate glass door. No more sightline of black spruce trees waving hello in the wind.

West of the house lay an additional seventy acres of field and forest, wild spreads of blackberry and raspberry, untended orchards emerging from odd thickets and completely wild apples, thorny and gnarled, yielding bitter or sweet or no fruit at all, a plethora of vegetation that, as a kid, I only thought of as bushes, as trees, but as an adult working in the horticulture industry I would learn to know by name: *cornus sericea, viburnum trilobum, picea glauca, populus tremuloides*. Piles of rocks, culled from the fields by generations of farmers, where Jaison and I would build stone forts, low walls and shaky battlements. Scattered remnants of rusted farm equipment like ancient relics of a forgotten world. An anthill the size of a Galapagos tortoise. A cow pond deep among the brambles. A bog of black muck where every spring, we'd harvest fiddleheads by the bushelful.

This is the world to which Jaison and I would retreat—every weekend, each day after school—to imagine ourselves warriors or wizards or Jedi, engaged unendingly in a battle to protect our home against invisible foes. This is where later I'd walk alone, trying to make sense of my head and my heart while smoking filched cigarettes and unruly amounts of pot. I composed my first poems and stories out here. I fantasized out here, and I escaped. In the winter, I followed rabbit tracks in the snow. This was the place I considered most my home. Among the ghosts of this land's previous inheritors. In the acute absence of anyone else.

fig. 8-10: my mother, 3x5 print on 110 film, August 1982.

In an obvious but effective pose, my mother sits in a throne-like wicker chair in our living room, the banister to the stairs visible over her left shoulder, a white ceramic lamp and, beyond that, the oval glass of our incongruously ornate front door unfocused beyond her right. Mum is wearing a sleeveless purple blouse with her long hair drawn in a loose pony-tail. She is smiling. It's a picture-taking smile, but a smile nevertheless. She looks beautiful.

Over her right breast, a lactation stain darkens a circle on her blouse. Unfortunate, maybe, but not unsurprising. Pink and ravenous, I would have been three months old.

An evident theme might be emerging. Between figures 8 and 9, Mum's expression is all that changes. Her eyes are wide. Her lips are parted. Her teeth are showing. Hers is a shock that blossoms into anger, as though the photo were taken mid-sentence: "What the fuck did you just say to me?"

*Figure 10 is taken at much closer range. So close that it's barely in focus. The word that comes to mind: **encroachment**. Mum's head and face. The neckline of her blouse. A bare crescent of shoulder. Her hair has come undone. The poise and smile of figure 8 are* *gone. So too is the lactation stain, now outside the frame. Everything in her expression is an exhausted plea. This is the face I know. So badly, she wants to be left alone.*

Again, I am certain my father took these pictures. They are exemplar of a trend I've witnessed over and over in the photos of my infanthood, in the four years between my birth and my parents' divorce. A shot of everyone smiling, followed by a shot of everyone confused or afraid, followed by a shot of anger, of disgust, of tears.

It's a trend I've seen repeated in photos of my father and his siblings, of his mother, California photographs taken by my grandfather. Everyone smiling. Everyone confused. Everyone hurt.

What was happening in the moments between the shutters' clicks?

What was being said?

Why did my male progenitors—what made them think—that this is how a family should appear?

After the divorce, very few pictures of the family were taken. As if the camera was an accessory to a serial crime (the complicity of documentation). As if no one anymore needed evidence of who we were, where we lived, what sorts of things were done.

IN THE FEW YEARS before I began writing *White Horses*—spurred partly by the encouragement of my professors in the English program at Alfred University and partly by some other, more discreet need—I took to writing personal essays about my family. Teased-free slivers of memory, resonant with the *feel* of importance yet explaining nearly nothing.

Black holes where I suspected certain truths lay hidden just beyond my grasp. Like this snapshot of my father, which was originally published in *Blue Moon*, a stapled-together 'zine out of Ithaca that, as far as I know, ceased publication a long time ago:

BRACKETT LAKE

Bound in fog, I sit with my father in our canoe upon a seemingly still lake. I am four, and the morning is silent. The water is grey, and the sky is grey and one with the depthless mists as we cast and reel and cast again, our lines disappearing ahead of us. Black shapes emerge from the mists surrounding, and I see turtles, immense, approaching slowly in formation. I panic and try to paddle away, but on my own the canoe only spins; my father tells me to cut it out, so I set down my paddle and wait, silently crying. It is only as we drift among them that I see that the turtles, swimming slowly, are only great stones, standing still. I can see where they touch bottom. The shore has been near all along.

Like so many of those early essays, the events of this story amount to little more than a few frames of excised film left on the editing room floor. I had no idea how or why this fit into the greater narrative of my life (I still don't). But I held tightly to this fleeting memory of being with my father, together on a lake. As if it might explain something about who I was, how I got to be me. As if it was a key, or a locked door.

But what about that moment was so important?

Was it the key, or was it the lock?

A better question might be: did this even happen?

Fragments that they were, those early personal essays count among my first publication credits (I guess the early '00s were a time when a lot people were trying to make sense out of little to no information). But there was an intrinsic limit to how much meaning I could hope to grope for in the dark. For at their heart, these stories were just elaborate questions. I'd eventually need to mine for some answers, dig up something concrete. Wondering wasn't enough. I would have to do the work.

It was on the strength of these essays that I earned a scholarship to the Salt Institute for Documentary Studies. My experiences at Salt would prove to be instrumental in how so much of my life has since played out. The city where I live. The stories I write. The people I call my friends. But for the purpose of this story, the number one lesson I learned was this:

Sometimes, the best way to nail down an answer is to simply ask the question.

I finished my work at Salt in December 2005. That following January, I asked my mother and father if they'd each agree to be interviewed. I would approach this as a professional. I would be objective and impartial. This is what I told myself. I would ask the questions I'd been afraid to ask, then stitch together the far-flung pieces into something like a whole.

It was worth a shot.

Of course, my aim was not my execution, my expectation not the reality. I asked my questions, but were the answers actually answers? Was it even possible for me to be impartial in this situation? Also: did I really *want* to be impartial? Was there even a sense or order to be made out of the material I'd gained?

I did the interviews and refined my notes. I attempted to reconstruct a narrative. But after months of struggling to decipher these pieces—the conflicting stories, the half-remembered details—I had to accept the bitter truth that some things can't ever be complete.

Shortly after setting the interviews aside, I began writing the first dream-like pieces of *White Horses*: an anti-novel of fragments that refuse to fit together.

This simple chronology—of, after years of struggling to make sense of the shapeless jigsaw puzzle of my past, I turn to fiction to explore the inner-life of a man who cannot tell the difference between his waking life and his dreams, his memories and his fantasies—makes for some pretty self-explanatory connective tissue. In the arena of non-fiction, I had tried and failed at this task. But the motivation remained. Perhaps in fiction, I could achieve something closer to success.

However, there is also this:

Throughout the whole process of rediscovering the following incomplete composite of interview transcriptions and reconstructions—which, for nearly a decade, I had forgotten I'd even written—as I edited and reread and battled with myself as to whether or not I should share this artifact from a life that feels so long past, told by a version (or versions) of me so young and so distant as to almost be a stranger, throughout all of this, a line from *White Horses* returned and returned again, sometimes as a taunt and sometimes as a warning but never as anything like an answer:

Is this something worth remembering?

—*Portland, Maine*
2015

II

(INTERVIEWS)

...every answer is a threat.

    —Bret Easton Ellis, *Lunar Park*

Let's imagine my life as an act of theater. A stage shaped like the inside of my head. Each actor portraying a version of me, speaking with or listening to different versions of me. In the shadows, my stenographer-self types quickly though ineffectually, missing lines and omitting notes on tone, improvising and ad-libbing. The stenographer is not to be trusted. I peer through the myopic windows of my eyes and recreate the outside world within. I interview again all the people I've interviewed. I relive everything I've already relived.

[The tape and recorder are on loan from a friend. Both are in rough shape, too often used and not necessarily tenderly: the recording is a mess of ambient hiss—the noise of silence—and a constant patter of low stereo thumping, perhaps the ghost beat of whatever was dubbed before.]

DOUGLAS:

So, just so that when I find this tape again thirty years down the road—"What the hell is this?"—so that I know what it is when I put it in the tape deck—

MUM:

Mm-hmm.

For too long, I've been writing stories that are in fact really questions artfully disguised as answers. Mapping the contours of my personal unknowns, the borderlands between memory and fantasy. An exercise in anxiety, in wondering, in never actually asking.

DOUGLAS:

—would you mind introducing yourself to the tape?

[*Her laugh is a smoker's laugh, dragged ruggedly up from her lungs like one length of slate skating unevenly over another.*]

This theater is my exercise in anxiety.

MUM:

Hello, Mr. Tape.

[We both laugh.]

The shadows within my skull melt and trickle to reform as a winter-lit room. The walls are green. The floors are hardwood, stained a luscious red. In one corner stands an enormous entertainment center, its TV on but muted, newscasters and experts speaking without sound. In the other corner, a bookshelf lined with manuals and guides, resources on fishing and Norway, on various American wars.

These are my father's books. But I own some of these same books, too.

From the shadows emerges a couch, upon which a version of me sits. Twenty-three years old. Blonde hair extending to my belt. Red beard resting on my chest. From the shadows emerges a reclining chair, upon which a different version of me takes a seat.

This latter version of me looks exactly like my father.

DOUGLAS:

You don't have to address it directly.

MUM:

Oh, I don't have to?

DOUGLAS:

No.

MUM:

Oh. [*Sighs through her teeth, a classic* sheesh.] I liked that.

> [*A bronze crab rests on the nightstand's pitted top. We're sitting on the bed in my former bedroom, the tape deck whirring between us on the bedspread. Same sea-green walls and grey carpet from my childhood. Same ink-stained desk. Same faint smell of patchouli and boy sweat. I've played G.I. Joes and listened to Black Sabbath on this bed. I've slept and fought with each of my serious girlfriends here. A huge rectangle of mirror inclines atop the dresser so that whenever I turn my head, I catch a glimpse of myself catching a glimpse of myself. My mother sits beside me like a plump little girl, grinning but nervous as she plays with her cigarette pack.*]

MUM:

I'm Donna Scott. Doug's mother. I don't know what else you want me to say. This is the year 2006. It's February and we're in Doug's bedroom. Having a little chat. *[Laughs.]* For all posterity. *[Dramatically:]* This moment is embedded in time.

In the winter of 2006, after completing my graduate semester at the Salt Institute for Documentary Studies, I requested a formal taped interview with each of my parents. Only my mother agreed. Bill suggested instead that we "get together and talk things out." He was insistent: there would be no tape deck, no record of events.

In this play that is my memory of talking with my father, in his living room in his home, there is nothing concrete, nothing for certain. Just memories stitched to memories. Endlessly refutable. No evidence to prove it ever happened.

DOUGLAS:

[Stumbling.] So I have, um, just. A few questions to ask. Mostly about you and my father. *[Tape breaks up.]* How did you meet my father?

MUM:

Oh [—*a downward sliding musical sound, a common preamble*—], let's see. The first recollection I have of your father. Out here in the driveway, a truckload of young fellers pulled in. And he was in the back of the truck [*laughs*] with some other ones. That was the first time I *really* remember meeting him. And they all jumped out and partied. [*Laughs.*] That was the times, the early '70s.

> [*It's mid-afternoon but the bedside lamp is on: a mellow glow. The sky outside's an iron bulkhead, stretching on for miles, letting no sunlight through.*]

It would be nearly a month after this interview with my mother before I drove to my father's house in coastal Maine. I arrived thinking we could sit down immediately and start our conversation. Instead, I helped him change the oil in his SUV. Lying beside him between the front tires with a pan to catch the dribbling black, I felt the ground solid with frost beneath me. While we worked, Bill kept saying, it was important that I know the truth, it was time finally that I know. At that point, it was all that he had to say.

DOUGLAS:

Was this when you were still with Tom [*Mum's first husband, the father of my brother Jaison and sister Tanya*]?

MUM:

Yep.

DOUGLAS:

So what year was this again?

MUM:

Oh, '74, maybe, '73?

DOUGLAS:

During the summer?

MUM:

Yeah, it was summertime. Because we talked about weeds.

Because there is no physical record of our conversation—no tape recording, no notes hastily scribbled in a pocket notebook—mostly what I remember are sensations and images. The bead of snot frozen in Bill's nostril while we worked outside. The grey light burnishing his red Old Town canoe behind the garage and the unfounded sense of togetherness I felt when we lifted to place it someplace safe from the elements. The silencing intimidation I felt whenever I tried to speak.

His hands always lay huge and heavy as the paws of a sleeping bear. His voice always hovered between a low croon and a threat.

DOUGLAS:

My father and you?

MUM:

Yep. We talked about edible weeds. Medicinal weeds. [*Beat.*] Weeds. [*And we laugh.*] Yep. He was interested in plantain for some reason, but I didn't know what it was. [*She pauses, remembers the moment.*] No, and it was growing all around our feet, I don't know if he was playing with me or what. [*She takes on a voice, one more akin to a backwoods old-timer* than the firm and halting tone that I know to be Bill's:] "Oh! You know anything about plantain?" [*And again in her own voice:*] "Yeah, I think it's a banana."

[*She laughs at her own joke, and I laugh with her. It seems perfectly natural for Mum to find herself entertaining.*]

MUM:

Yeah, no, that wasn't what he was talking about. He never did point it out to me, so maybe he didn't know it, either.

DOUGLAS:

[*Haltingly—I can never spit things out:*] He probably would have been pretty young then, huh?

MUM:

Yeah, probably eighteen, nineteen.

[*The tape breaks up in a wash of hiss and low puttering.*]

The first question asked was by my father to me.

"So what *do* you remember?"

We were sitting in his living room, just in from working on his car. He had poured himself a glass of ice water from the kitchen, was holding it cupped between his large hands like a sliver of chilling fire. I don't remember if I had a glass, too. I felt disarmed by the lingering cold, and the answer I gave, I think, is what shaped everything that followed.

"Not much," I lied. "Barely anything at all."

He nodded, slowly but not breaking eye contact, perhaps aware—perhaps contented—that I'd just given him license to say whatever he pleased.

"You ought to know the truth." He turned a wrench and let the oil jet free. "It's time you know the truth."

MUM:

I just kinda knew he liked me because, whenever I went out, whenever Tom and I went out somewhere, Tom would just leave me. And Bill was always there.

When asked, Bill claimed not to remember meeting my mother for the first time. But many things are easy to forget. From what I've seen, of pictures taken during the 1970s, my mother was a short and trim woman with dark braids that hung over her shoulders. She was a pretty young woman with an easy eagerness to smile, to laugh, to play. Bill couldn't think of one reason why he might have been interested in her.

MUM:

I can't remember, initially, how we got together. [*Pause.*] I don't remember. [*Pause.*] I think we had lunch together a couple times. I'd make up a lunch or something and he'd come pick me up and we'd go up on Westford Hill or something. And that's initially how it started.

> [*It will be some time before I realize: I have given both of my parents' permission to play the same game. By claiming falsely that I remember nearly nothing, I allow Bill to say whatever he may please. Just as in this moment, in countless moments to follow, I allow Mum to fill the gaps in her memory with vague anecdotes, plausible suppositions that perhaps I should be questioning. It is a problem I fail to identify until far too late: I entered the conversation already distrusting Bill's account. Why did I not treat Mum's story with an equal degree of skepticism?*]

After a long pause, Mum continues.]

MUM:

And I don't know what else to tell you. That's about what we did.
Then we started going out. Having drinks. Stuff like that. And then
he moved in. *[Long pause.]* I wish I could remember what year that
was. I can't remember. *[Long pause.]* Probably '79.

*[My parents got together during the spring of 1979. Jaison would have
been four. Tanya, nine. The proceedings for Mum's divorce from her first
husband, Tom, were in their final month. My father, meanwhile, was
exiting a relationship of his own. As Mum recalls it, on the night of his
breakup, Bill had gone out on the town hoping to find my mother. Mum
was likewise looking for him. Yet each was at a different bar, looking in
the wrong place for the other.]*

DOUGLAS:

So, when you were still with Tom, and [Bill] would come around
and talk to you, it wasn't that you knew that he liked you, it—

MUM:

Oh, I liked him, too. And of course, Tom was being shitty to me all the time. [*Laughs.*] That's what he'd do, leave me with somebody. [*Laughs.*] Smart.

> [*But again, too late, I have to question: Why was Tom being shitty? In what way? Was it possible Mum was being shitty right back? After all, what husband relaxes joyously while observing his wife seduce and be seduced by a younger man? What wife leaves her husband for another man without recognizing the hurt she's inflicting?*
>
> *Of course, the details are irrelevant. What matters is that already, before my parents become romantic, there is a precedent of hurt, of acting out of hurt, of indifference to someone else's hurt.*]

MUM:

But anyway. Yeah. It's like. Not only was my marriage with Tom not going on very good grounds. When I was out and about, which was rare because I rarely got out of here, but when I was out and about, Bill was always there. [*Pause.*] And he listened to me. And all those nice things that people do before they get married. [*Laughs.*] Actually hear what you're saying. Considerate. Help you, indoors and outdoors and all that good stuff.

For years, I'd been asking Bill to tell me his version of things. He always put it off. "You're not old enough yet." I first asked him when I was twenty-one years old.

This condescension has traced an unignorable boundary-line through nearly all my adult interactions with Bill. Whether consciously or otherwise, my father's chronic need to prove himself superior, correct, justified, has been an ever-expanding wedge between us. It creates a distance in moments when we should each be trying to come closer together. As have a great many other things.

Just as today—in his February living room recreated in my tiny theater—Bill said as preamble that his truth of things would probably confuse and disturb me, would be nothing I'd heard before. "I hope," he said, trying to smile but sneering smugly instead, "that you can take it."

DOUGLAS:

So what interested you in him, what attracted you to him?

MUM:

Oh, well he was paying attention to me, and I wasn't getting any attention anywhere else. Here with kids all day. Kids and kids and kids. He was another adult voice. And he was cute. Shit. [*Laughs.*] He was nice to me. Made me feel [*pause*], you know, like I wasn't an old dishrag. And so, we both liked each other and both knew it, but it was just like...

[*She trails off, fills her cheeks with air, slowly lets out her breath in a prolonged and weary **shush**. Claps her hands against her thighs. Recites some anecdotal evidence involving people and places—friends and bars—that no longer exist, no longer bear any meaning. Then she finally says the thing she's been meaning to say all along:*]

MUM:

And of course, when you're in a bad marriage, too, you can fantasize about things. Makes you feel not so useless.

[*When Mum first said these words—as I listened later to the tape over and over again, laying down the transcript of our conversation—I felt only commiseration: I, too, have invited the worst kind of trouble upon myself simply by putting faith in my fantasies. Convinced that people loved me. Certain I was protected. I took it as one more thing*]

I'd inherited from my mother. It made us weaker, but it also made us alike.

But what fantasy was Bill buying into? What was happening to sour his current relationship that convinced him that Mum was the way out? What long black storm cloud did he believe—ultimately wrongly—he was crawling out from under?

Some questions, you never have the chance to ask. They likely don't have answers anyway. By the end of that summer, Mum and Bill were living together in my mother's farmhouse.]

In our interview, Bill could not remember meeting my mother, could not remember their first dates, could not remember staying up all night talking with her, or being surprised by her, or being at work and wishing to be in her arms or eyes or body instead, or any of the other things that occur at the beginning of a relationship between two people who eventually will love one another. Those things that tend to be imbedded in a person's mind—the first time one cooked dinner for the other, the first time naked hands touched—are completely absent from his memory. He lived with a woman in town, then lived with another in the country. Nothing in between mattered.

There likewise was no progression of events. "Your mother was just a bitter person." From marriage to not-marriage. "Snide and vindictive. A person can live with that for only so long."

He said this as though he were the one who precipitated the divorce.

As if I didn't know that she was the one who left him.

Still cold from the wind and frost outside, my fingers lay numb and aching in my lap. Stones or fish or tiny bones found buried in ice. This is one version of my memory.

DOUGLAS:

And how much longer before you were married?

MUM:

I married in '81. When I was pregnant with you.

DOUGLAS:

So you guys didn't get married until after Danny?

[*My brother. Who died at birth. Never gasping a single breath of air. In this moment, still resting as ash in a box beneath Mum's bed.*]

MUM:

Right, didn't get married 'til I was pregnant with you.

DOUGLAS:

So you were with my father for probably, what, six years then? You got divorced in—when did you guys get divorced?

MUM:

'86.

[*I'd have been four. Jaison, eleven. Tanya, sixteen.*]

DOUGLAS:

When did things start changing?

MUM:

Well, things started changing like when…. [*She pauses, swallows, takes a breath and starts over.*] It was after you were born. [*Beat.*] Although, you know sometimes I think back. And maybe they started changing before that. It was like after you were born he had a whole different attitude. Before? Jaison and Tanya wanted to call him Dad.

[*Really?*]

MUM:

They all got along great.

[Really?]

MUM:

And then once you were born—and see, once we were married he treated me different. There was an immediate change, like I was a piece of property. The feeling I had was like now he had a deed to me. It was so subtle but so weird. And then his attitude toward Tanya and Jaison changed totally once you were born.

[*Again, I am giving her too much allowance. Bill changed. I was the cause. But how did she change after I was born? What catalyzing actions and attitudes did Mum adopt that she cannot or will not name?*]

DOUGLAS:

How so?

MUM:

[*As though she cannot find any other word:*] He was *mean*. It was like a *mean* streak, like there was just something *mean* coming out of him, and that's the way I felt about his relationships with a lot of people. Just like he always saw the bad side and he was cruel and mean about it. 'Member like Susan and Wendell come over one day and Tanya went running out. She loved Wendell, Wendell had known her since she was a little baby, and she was out there just jibber-jabbering about something, I think she was about twelve. And, um. They were jibber-jabbering as they were coming in the house, she was all excited telling him something and Bill says, "Oh, just get out of here. No one wants to listen to you anyway." And [*Wendell and Susan*] stopped and said, "We do. We were listening to her."

> [*If Tanya had been twelve, this would have happened the year I was born.*]

46

"In that way," he said, "she was a lot like my mother." And after a short pause. "You know, you're a lot like your mother, too."

I nodded. "Of course I am." I didn't intend to, but I counterattacked. "She raised me."

Again, without my realizing, I've redirected our dialog. My goal was to be open and understanding. I was convinced: I am being open and understanding. Yet here I am, guaranteeing that Bill and I are at odds. Not deflecting his barbs at all, but sailing them straight back.

Bill turned away toward the silent TV. The subject dropped. I sat still in my seat across from him and waited, my silence allowing me to pretend it didn't matter how Bill had just used Mum as a weapon against me. Pretending this wasn't the inverse of an echo. Something I'd heard too many times.

When I was a teenager, and Mum and I would get into fights about something—anything—the argument could end so easily, so predictably, Mum's emotional atomic bomb:

"Jesus," she would say, face red, words filtered through gnashing teeth, "you are *just* like your *father*."

This was before Bill and I ever talked, before I would even suspect that he might be a person, a human, something more than a vicious monster. In my mind then, he was a violent and silent shadow from the murkiness of my past. And in my mother's eyes, I was just like him.

DOUGLAS:

Did you ever confront him about it?

MUM:

That never went anywhere. That just never went anywhere. You didn't confront Bill. There was no listening. There was his way. That was it. [*She pauses, slaps her hands to her thighs.*] Try and confront Jaison about something he doesn't want to. You can't. He don't want to talk about it, you're not gonna talk about it. And that's the way Bill was, too.

Early on, I considered asking my brother for an interview. The idea was immediately rejected. I didn't need to ask him to know there were some things he would never be able to say.

Yet earlier this week, Jaison stopped by for the night. He was passing through from one place to another and needed somewhere to stay. Standing on the steps outside of my apartment, smoking and drinking and watching his black dog sniff around the neighborhood, Jaison turned to me and said, "There's a lot of shit I'm still pissed off about, you know? For the most part, I let it go, just let it go and not think about it. But sometimes Mum and me'll be talking, and it'll all come back. Especially if I've been drinking." His hand flexes and relaxes along the neck of his beer bottle, flexes and relaxes. "Things I'm still pissed at her for." Raising his cigarette to his lips, Jaison looks away from me, watches his dog circle and circle in the dark. "Some shit won't ever be resolved."

This is the closest Jaison and I have ever come to discussing any of these things. It was the first time that I realized that some of that latent rage that's seethed inside him all these years might be aimed at more than one person, at more than one series of events.

But of course, this too is another act of theater. Artfully shaped to fit my agenda.

What am I forgetting?

What am I omitting?

[From here, the conversation diverges from the facts to Mum's speculation as to what might have precipitated Bill's change in demeanor. Her theories are plausible, but they're also unfounded. Then she segues into a few episodes from my childhood, about how I once called a leech a "mothersucker," how I once peed on an electric fence.]

MUM:

Or the time you wanted to—[*She pauses, restarts.*] Beal Bean scratched you. And there you were tugging that great big cat up the stairs. "Where you goin', Doug?" "I'm gonna throw Beal Bean out the window!" [*She laughs: slate on slate.*] And you were gonna.

> *[This episode, I actually remember. But it's part of a game both Mum and Bill play, each telling stories that I might or might not remember, stories most likely lost in my childhood's foggy prehistory. Any detail I might provide is invariably wrong. In my own stories, I am the least reliable narrator.*
>
> *Side A ends here. The rattling sound of my hands on the recorder, search-ing for the stop button, then the pop and silence of the recording's end, immediately followed by Tony Bennett singing about how you ought to know now.*
>
> *Begin Side B.]*

DOUGLAS:

[*After a deep preliminary sigh:*] So you and Bill got separated a couple times—

MUM:

Yep.

DOUGLAS:

—between when I was maybe two and four?

MUM:

Yep.

DOUGLAS:

What was going on that caused you to separate?

MUM:

Um. First I was getting...getting a lot of.... Tanya was saying that there was a lot of things going on that I was missing. That he was doing things to her. So I started being very watchful and I found that she was certainly looking, he was looking like she was saying.

[*Stops, regroups.*] I never actually saw him...do...you know, anything *really* bad, but I did catch him...lying her in positions that she should have never been doing. I don't know how else to say that.

> [*Mum stops speaking. There are a few techniques I learned at Salt for dealing with moments like these. You can let the silence stretch on without interruption, giving your subject the time and space they need in order to resume what they'd been meaning to say. You can also ask something indirect but connected, delicately teasing free the thread snarling their emotions and tying their tongue.*]

DOUGLAS:

What was he doing?

> [*Or you can be an asshole and ask the painful question pointblank.*]

MUM:

Bending her backwards over the sink and putting his body up against her.

> [*Mum is not looking at me anymore while she speaks, is looking down and through her hands folded like sleeping birds in her lap. After a long pause, she resumes, her voice low and husky and quiet.*]

MUM:

And she was telling me a lot of other things. I remember the period as just being dark and depressing. Because it was my daughter and my husband. I knew that wasn't going to work.

DOUGLAS:

And this was when Tanya was thirteen, fourteen?

[Mum only nods.]

DOUGLAS:

So you guys got separated then. But you also got back together.

MUM:

Well, then, we got separated and then...Bill's sister took Tanya out there [to California, where Bill was born, where he spent the early years of his life, where most of his family still lives] and kept her for the summer. So that never got dealt with is what it all amounted to. [She coughs.] I couldn't get rid of him anyway. He was here all the time. Just, he wouldn't leave.

[Again, that echo: "when I was out and about, Bill was always there."]

MUM:

He left, but he didn't leave, you know what I mean? And that was
in the summer.

> [Tanya has alluded to these things, but never directly spoken of them
> to me. Again, my own cowardice keeps me from asking too much too
> forwardly. I fear that my urge to know more about my family—to draw in
> closer to whom each really is—will in turn alienate them from me. Just
> in writing this, I fear I'm pushing them away.]

DOUGLAS:

When was the next time you were separated?

MUM:

It was a year later, and that was it. See, I get the two times mixed
up in my head, I can't... [Pause.] Things that happened. But I know
the last, when I finally decided I'd had it, was when we had the big
freak-out out here. You know what I mean. With the shovel and
the whole works. [She's smoking now, her inhalations and exhalations
punctuating her speech.] Do you know what I mean?

DOUGLAS:

I, I—

MUM:

I don't know how much of that you remember.

[Nor do I.]

DOUGLAS:

That was one of the things I wanted to ask you about.

I asked Bill about his childhood in California—about being the youngest of three children, about watching the painful breakup of his parents at such a young age—but he claimed to remember none of it. "I've good reason," he said, "to forget a lot of my childhood." But isn't purposefully forgetting the same as pretending not to remember, to in fact not forget at all? Avoidance in the guise of moving on.

"What about the truck accident?" I asked. I had learned from my grandmother that, when Bill was a young boy, a large delivery truck of some sort went off the road and burst through the chain-link surrounding the playground where Bill was playing. Bill had been standing next to the fence: it pinned him to the ground when the truck came through, trapping him between the playground gravel and the engine's mechanical breath. "You don't remember any of that, either?"

Bill tried to keep his gaze on me, his expression plain and unchanged—as though, by putting on the façade of calm unaffectedness, he would remain calmly unaffected—but he eventually turned away. His face softened, the lines around his eyes relaxing as he gazed abstractedly at the air before him. For the first time in my life, my father actually looked vulnerable.

"I remember," he said, "there was a man who talked to me. While I was under the truck, waiting for help, there was a man who talked to me. I don't know who he was. But he waited with me until help arrived."

Just as quickly as the change came over him, Bill looked back at me, fixed his eyes and mouth in a shape of smug omniscience. Wherever he'd been—whatever place my question had sent him—he'd abandoned. A part of me wished that he had never left it behind.

"And I was angry at my mother," he concluded, "for letting it happen," and in his tone, it was clear, that anger had never gone away.

DOUGLAS:

What I remember, um. What seemed at the time to have been the last straw, as far as what *I* was seeing, was when he squeezed Beal Bean...

MUM:

...and threw him up against the wall.

DOUGLAS:

Which...What I actually remember of that day has absolutely nothing to do with any of that. I just remember walking down the stairs at one point

[in a white T-shirt, in a pair of action figure underpants]

and you and Jaison and Tanya were downstairs, and you were looking for Beal Bean or something,

[like I'm reciting from a dream]

I remember everyone was concerned about Beal Bean, and I walk down the stairs and into the kitchen where Bill was. And then I remember walking *out* of the kitchen and Bill was still sitting at the table, I think he was eating breakfast, maybe drinking orange juice, and he said something about Mr. T. From the A-Team? And I was like, "Yeah, Mr. T." Because I liked Mr. T. And that's all I really remember of that day.

[A brief pause as Mum moves her tongue inside her mouth, as if tasting for something that isn't there.]

MUM:

I don't think *that* is even the same day.

Bill, too, did not remember this happening. Par for the course.

MUM:

Because when things all— [*She pauses, starts again.*] It was first thing in the morning. And he and I had that bedroom over there [*she points over her shoulder, through the wall and to the unused bedroom on the other side of the stairway.*] Beal Bean jumped up and was lying beside me and he was purring, and your father kept going like that [*she flicks her finger quickly at the air, as if pinging a bug harshly away*] to his nose. And I said, "Leave the damn cat alone." So he punched me in the face.

"Until the end of the marriage," Bill said, sipping his glass of ice water, "I never raised a hand against your mother. And even then, it was in self-defense."

The afternoon sun poured through the great glass doors leading to his backyard, trickling across the house to dance duskily with the ice cubes, filling his glass with light. Chilling fire.

"You punched her in the face," I said, no longer asking but reciting what I took as fact. "In bed. The last morning you two were married." I watched him, feeling hollow and still as a nutshell emptied of its seed. "Right?" I breathed slowly through paper lungs. "Right?"

I had come here to ask questions. But I was pushing. It doesn't matter who started it. We were pushing and pushing back.

Bill set down his glass on the table. "That's a lie." The ice cubes tinked and popped. "That's a goddamn lie."

MUM:

And he picked the cat up and threw it against the wall. But when he picked the cat up and threw him against the wall, you seen it, 'cause you were in that little room beside ours. And you seen it. And you were all freakin' out because he threw your cat. And later, when he was living [down state], you had asked him about it—at least this is what you told me, when you came home from being down there. You asked him why he did that to your cat, and he said a bad man did it, somebody, a burglar came in and did it.

DOUGLAS:

I remember that. [*And again, more quietly:*] I remember that.

The weekends I spent with Bill during that time were filled with burglars. Hiding in shadows. Keeping me in line. Just beyond the periphery of the yard when I played outside. In the bathroom of any restaurant. In my memories of our visits together, I feared everything beyond Bill's hand holding mine.

DOUGLAS:

So what *did* happen after he punched you and threw the cat?

MUM:

I got dressed—Tanya had to go to work, so I got her up and you guys, you and Jaison got dressed and I called the police. And he was in there making coffee. And I called the police and they said, "Do you want to press charges?" And I said, "Uh [—*she pauses, just as she must have paused on the line twenty years before, weighing the uncertainties of her options, then speaks carefully, choosing each word—*], I don't really think I want to do that." They said, "Well, there's nothing we can do. But you ought to get yourself *out* of there." So I put you guys all in the car—I had to take Tanya to work, into the Park View Terrace.

> [*During the next few minutes of tape, Mum tries to remember what exactly happened for the rest of that day: where she and I and Jaison went, who we stayed with, how we got from one place to another. In this way, she and I are both alike, mixing up details and forgetting the order of events, to the point where we no longer trust our memories but only the feeling—the emotional experience—of that time.*
>
> *The only certain detail is that it was the April Sunday when Daylight Savings*

Time ended. The clocks should have been set ahead, but weren't. So Tanya was late for work, and Mum was late picking her up at the end of the day. It has the feel of critical symbolism, but not the necessary depth: all day, we were running on a clock and time set differently than the rest of the world.]

MUM:

Then we went and picked up Tanya. We had to find a place to stay. And Tanya was freaking out, she needed clothes [*for school*]. So we came back here—I called first. [*No one answered.*] We pulled in here and. [*The pause is brief, but noticeable: her sentence ends abruptly as she descends back into it.*] [*Tanya*] jumped out, and I locked the door, and she went in to get some clothes. And [*Bill*] was hiding somewhere, he had hidden his truck. And I don't know where in the hell he was, but all of a sudden, he was there and he was in the car. And he grabbed you and went into the house.

"I wasn't hiding. I was sitting on the back porch when you guys all came home. And Tanya ran inside to get some drugs."

Why he added this last footnote is beyond me. I had already told him—on various occasions—that I have used and enjoyed a variety of different drugs. Why would I care if, all those years past, Tanya had run inside to grab her stash instead of some clothes for school? Perhaps, for a moment, Bill still thought he was trying to convince a judge of something that, all these years later, no longer mattered.

"I thought you had all come home for the night, so I went out to the car to get you. And suddenly it was a game of tug of war. I didn't want to hurt you, so I let you go."

A long silent moment passed before I realized he'd finished. His story ended here.

[Mum recites as if from a dream.]

MUM:

And he did it when Tanya was coming out 'cause it was like she was in the middle of it for some reason, she was coming out with the stuff—*No!* It was Jaison grabbed Beal Bean, he didn't want to leave him there. You and him were crying about leaving Beal Bean, and so Jaison opened the door to grab Beal Bean and out of nowhere, Bill was in the car and he grabbed you and went into the house. And Tanya grabbed you and then it became a crazy fight. Well anyway, he ended up in the house and he had locked the door. And I got out of that car and—'cause I was sitting in there with it running, waiting for her to come out when that all happened—and I kicked that door right in. You were standing right there, *and your eyes were so big!* And I picked you up and started going out and that's when Bill grabbed Tanya and he was trying to throw her down the cellar stairs. So I put you down and I grabbed her, I got her just by—'cause she had a dress on, a skirt, I got her. I think it ripped the skirt, but I did get her enough so that I could pull her up, she was on her way down. And then from there, she went to call the police, he went and ran after her and took the telephone apart, just—I can remember things happening but the order.... Jaison kept coming in and saying, "What can I do, what can I do?" I'd say, "Get in the car, at least then I'll know *you're* there." And one time he came in and was, "What can I do, what can I do?" and you were just standing there so he grabbed you and put you in the car. [*At this, we both laugh, perhaps because—at least in my memory—this has always been Jaison's role, to grab me and remove me from danger while the rest of the world falls apart.*] So Tanya and I took off and we were getting in the car, well Bill grabbed me and pulled me down. [*No more laughter.*] And he was trying to wrap the telephone cord around my neck. So I told Tanya, "Get in the car, get the hell out of here." But she couldn't drive it because it was a stick shift. So. She kept trying to and it kept—[*She stutters, losing her way, tries to find it again and in doing so comes out of her dream, her voice finding its usual sardonic edge.*] He was trying to push my head under the tires. He was being a real asshole.

> [*Every time I listen to this tape–and even then, sitting across from her– I'm shocked by the audacity of her understatement. My father has created a situation wherein either he strangles Mum, or my sister–in her attempt to escape–crushes our mother's head. Thus leading to the obvious conclusion: "He was being a real asshole."*]

MUM:

And I was fighting him off, doing whatever I could to keep him away from you kids and hoping that she could get the car started and get the hell out of there and I finally I was all in and I just sat down on the steps. Panting. And I looked up and he reached into his pocket and pulled out the set of keys he had and he started turning back and he was on his way in[*to the car*]. And I turned around and I looked down and there was that [*coal*] shovel that Terry Anderson gave me from the B&A Railroad. And I took up that goddamn shovel and *BAM!* He came rolling out of that car, I slammed the car door. [*She laughs, more than a little sadistically.*] I wanted to hit him again. Really, I wanted to take his head and just pop it all the way across the lawn. But I just got in the car and got the hell out of there.

[Mum rolls the low-burnt tip of her cigarette in the ashtray on the bed-side stand. The ashtray has legs and is open on a hinge like a gaping metal mouth. She stabs out the cigarette and flips the lid shut over the ashes: the ashtray becomes a bronze crab. Its belly is warm with cinders.

That night, we stayed at a safe place just a few towns away. The next morning, Mum filed for divorce.]

MUM:

I wasn't changing my mind this time.

"And that was it?"

"That was it."

"Didn't you try to throw Tanya down the stairs? And strangle Mum with the phone cord?"

"*She* tried to strangle *me*." He paused, looked away. "I think she bit me, too. Very immature."

I bit him in the back, too, when he was fighting with Tanya. I couldn't get him away—get him off of Tanya, he was beating on her. I bit him in the back. Through his T-shirt and sweatshirt and stuff but. [*She pooches out her lips and nods.*] I felt my teeth meet.

The silence dragged on as I waited for him to continue, to fill the gaps in his too-brief account. But there was no budging. Even though he'd indirectly admitted there'd been a fight—"*She* tried to strangle *me*...she bit me, too"—he still believed he could pretend naïvely that none of it had happened. Bill made a smacking sound with his lips as though he were tasting his mouth, sipped his water, slowly blinked his eyes like an animal before a nap.

"Do you have any regrets," I finally asked, "about anything that happened during that period in your life?"

I was hoping he would wish to take back all the violence and hatred, all the sinister games and shows of power, all the things to which he had yet to admit having done or had done to him. Examining his fingernails, he said, "I probably played too rough with Jaison. Wrestling and such. All innocent games, but clearly too much for a boy his age."

I can remember—after the divorce, when Bill would come to pick me up for his custodial weekends—standing in the front yard beside Jaison and watching the color drain from his face as Bill came rolling down the road to the house, his car donned in a great cape of dust rising from the hard-packed earth. Later, when he was older, Jaison would grow red and trembling, eyes burning and wet, not so much crying as overwhelmed with impotent rage. Eventually, he snapped and screamed for Bill to leave, leave, leave our house and lives and leave, leave, leave.

Whatever happened between Jaison and Bill that could cause such hurt and fury is beyond me. It's not that I don't understand. It's that the knowledge is not mine to have. Jaison will not talk about his childhood as it relates to my father. It's not anything he can talk about. And I do not want to force him to remember.

"Actually," Bill added, almost as an afterthought—almost as though it's all he ever meant to say, "I really only regret ever meeting your mother."

"Really?" A cold stone rode low inside me. "The whole relationship?"

"Yes."

"And everything it entailed?"

"Yes."

"So you regret that I was born?"

Mum had her particular emotional atomic bomb. Apparently, so did Bill.

"Douglas, if I had married a different woman and had had a son with her instead, would that boy be any less you than you are?"

I didn't have to wonder long about this question. Bill answered it himself. He spread his hands plaintively—sorry, kid!—and raised his shoulders in a shrug.

MUM:

I know I hurt him. But that didn't stop him one bit. It was like he didn't even know I was there. Didn't feel it, didn't. The only thing that stopped him then was Tanya took his glasses off, threw 'em. And that kinda pissed him off, he went after his glasses. [*She* tries to laugh, but the laugh turns into a cough, ragged and wet, ending in two pronounced jolts.] I'm sure Tanya remembers other things.

[The one time Tanya and I talked about this we were in Reno, sitting on her bed and each only half-awake. We had both just awoke from afternoon naps, had just gotten high in her basement apartment, and however we got onto the subject is lost somewhere between dreams and smoke. Maybe she just started talking, unprovoked, just speaking what was on her mind.

"Do you remember the shovel fight? Back when we were kids?"

"No." Then slowly, as if it were my first, I drew in a sharp breath. "Yes. I do remember." I had forgotten. Until she asked, I had forgotten.

As if a sorrowful but catchy song played somewhere in the back of her mind, she rhythmically nodded her head. "Yeah. Pretty fucked up, huh?" And she took another hit off her pipe.]

Suddenly, Bill's demeanor changed. He turned to face me directly, leaned one elbow against the arm of his chair. An intentness narrowed his eyes, like if he peered hard enough, he could see through the hair and skin and bones of my face and look directly into my mind.

"Why do you want to know all of this? What does it matter to you?"

And a moment later:

"Why do you keep coming here?"

And then:

"What is it that you're looking for, Douglas?"

But both of us knew, already, it was too late.

"I don't know, Bill."

Proof that you're more than you are. Proof that you want to be forgiven.

"I don't know."

Too late because there is no proof. No proof because what I want isn't true.

[From this point on, the interview shifts into an associative ramble. Pubs and restaurants that no longer exist. People who moved away, went to jail, or died before I was old enough to ever remember meeting them.

She tells me how, divorced from her and bound by a restraining order, Bill would still come around the house and cause trouble for everyone. Throwing silverware around the kitchen. Stealing the license plates off her car. Doing whatever he could to make life hard for her. Again, again: "I couldn't get rid of him.... He left, but he didn't leave."]

From my short time studying documentary writing and journalism, I knew that even the most pointless of interviews should end with the same question. "Thanks for your time, Bill. Is there anything else you'd like to add, any questions you'd like to ask me?"

He thought for a moment before answering. "Why do you call me 'Bill'? Why don't you call me 'Dad'?"

Looking back, I cannot help but recognize how sweetly naïve Bill was in asking this. As if he could not possibly understand how hurtful he's been. In this conversation. Over my entire life. Shouldn't the answer be obvious?

But still. He asked. As far as I can recall, my response was the first time I ever spoke openly and directly to my father. In all likelihood, it will never happen again.

"Because," I said, my voice low and even, somewhere between a croon and a threat, "'Dad' is a term given in affection from a son to his father. It requires more than simple biology. It requires love, and familiarity. It requires a relationship. But you're a stranger to me, Bill. You treat me coolly, and keep me at a distance. You've done nothing to earn that name."

Bill maintained his smug grin and nodded. But he didn't say anything for a long, long time. Finally, clapping his hands like a meaty bell signaling the end of yet another day, he said to me, genial and polite as any telephone operator, "I'm glad we had this little chat."

DOUGLAS:

I think that's pretty much everything I had meant to ask.

MUM:

Yeah, I thought you were more interested in what went on with

the.... When we talked before, you mentioned the custody suit....
Well of course, that's all a matter of record.

A matter of record. What Bill told me was neither new nor confusing. It was disappointing and old. It was the same story he told in court twenty and fifteen years before, at the divorce and custody hearings. It was the same story I heard second-hand from Mum and Tanya and my grandmother—Bill's own mother—as they recalled it at the time. After all these years, his story has remained exactly the same. A denial of all wrongdoing. An innocent man baffled by his hysterical, delusional wife.

I have considered requesting from the court a copy of the stenographer's transcript from both proceedings, but have likewise decided not to bother. How many times can I hear the same story, one that never adds up, one that never conclusively concludes?

DOUGLAS:

Was there anything else *you* wanted to say?

MUM:

No. [*There's an irony in her laugh, as if there's nothing left to say, as if she never wanted to say any of what she's said. The world could carry on and end in silence now. Shush.*] No, nothing really that I *need* to say. See, I don't know how much of anything you remember anyway. You may remember a lot more than you think you do.

> [*This comment seems as though it might lead to something more, but it goes nowhere, hangs in the air that hisses like rain on pavement. A moment later, the tape ends. The interview with my mother is over.*]

So what do I remember?

I remember leaving Bill's house that day feeling as though part of me—my eyes, my hands—had awakened from some fog of dream while the rest of me—my head, my heart—remained lost in the nonsense of that same depressing grey. He hugged me before I left his house, and I felt disgusted at myself for letting him hug me. I remember driving home in this fog, barely conscious of my passage through time and space like a bullet among other bullets. I remember wondering which one of us had been rejected by the other.

I don't remember if, when Bill hugged me, I hugged him back. I don't remember saying anything by means of goodbye.

And I don't remember seeing Beal Bean hit the wall. But I do remember the thump. I don't remember seeing anyone hurting anyone. The head beneath the tire. Teeth sinking into shoulder. But I remember my brother and sister huddled around me, terrified, inside the car. And I remember the screams. And the screams. And the screams.

I remember, just weeks after she filed for divorce, sitting on the living room floor with Mum on one side of me and Jaison on the other, the three of us together like a living triangle with our old black rotary telephone centered between us. The same phone Bill had disassembled with his great and nimble paws, whose cord he used to strangle Mum. With this weapon, now a tool, between us, Mum and Jaison taught me how to use the telephone. They gave me two numbers to memorize, and made sure I had them right. The numbers I learned were not for the police, or the fire department, or for the ambulance—these would come later. The numbers they had me memorize were my father's. One for the chainsaw repair shop he owned in town. One for his new apartment. They were giving me an electric connection to my father. They were giving the thing they needed to protect—the soft and vulnerable core to their suddenly violent and trustless world—the means to contact their enemy. I can only imagine how that must have felt to them.

I remember standing beside Jaison on the front steps of the house while he yelled at Bill standing in the driveway, yelling for him to leave, fuck off, go away. I remember yelling with him. I yelled, "Bill, please leave." As far as I remember, this was the first time I ever called him by his name. Yet I do not remember the last time I called him "Dad."

Yes, I remember sometimes not wanting to visit with my father, but I also remember sometimes wanting to see him. I couldn't understand how the family I loved—my mother, my brother, my sister—could all hate this man that I loved. And I likewise could not understand how my father could in turn hate my family. It was confusing. And it was terrifying. How could the two halves of my life hate each other so incredibly? How could I love both?

Eventually, I did not love both sides. When Bill lost his suit for custody of me, he disappeared. He did not call me, or write to me, or drop by to visit me. He vanished from my life, as if one of us had been erased. He has since given me a variety of reasons for having done this—once even reminding me that the phone works both ways—but the explanation that sounds most plausible is one issued, of all the biased parties involved, by my grandmother. "When the court ruled in your mother's favor," she told me, voice wrecked from decades of cigarette smoke, "your mother got full custody. If Bill wanted to see you, he would have had to ask her." And in her old throat, she made a sound that might have been a laugh, or a groan, or sigh. "My son is too proud to ask for anything like permission."

I love my grandmother. I remember always loving my grandmother. I've learned more about my father from her than from anyone else. She was the one who first planted the notion in me that Bill might be more than a collection of violent stories, more than a dark presence and a sudden absence. He was once a loving husband, once a clever young man, once a quiet little boy. The last time she saw her son was during the custody hearings. She was testifying on my behalf. She testified against Bill. She did not believe her own son to be an adequate parent for me, and as punishment for this, Bill erased her from his life. Yet she still loved him, and as far as I know, loves him still. This is something else she has taught me: how to love when you're given no reason to love.

Which is not to say that I love my father. Nor does it mean I hate him. Sometimes it seems as though those two extremes have mellowed over time, have become some colorless middle ground of acceptance, worthy of no emotional experience. I have fingers. I have language. I have blood and a history in my blood. I have thick hair on my face and scalp. I am sometimes helpless but to laugh like a maniac rolling on the floor and sometimes helpless but to remain still for hours, staring into space, hoping this day will finally, finally end. I have an artform and a car and a birthmark on my hip. And I have a father.

Yet such neutral acceptance is far from the truth, too. Because it changes. Sitting in his living room and speaking with Bill about these things—recreating this moment again and again in my mind—everything changes. Sometimes I'm cold with despairing realization. Sometimes I'm indignant and enraged. Sometimes I'm grasping. Sometimes I'm afraid. But I'm never firm. I'm never concrete. Because nothing ever remains the same.

Except for Bill's story. Bill's story refuses to change.

An unchanged story confesses an unchanged teller. Despite all my hopes, Bill is the same man he has always been, will always be. He denies what he doesn't like, and what he admits to, he feels no remorse for.

Meanwhile, I regret even telling this story, for even having this story to tell. I'm tired of hearing it, tired of thinking it over like a riddle I can't ever solve. Hopeless. But I go over it again. Just one more time. And the time after that, too. And in each retelling in this theater empty but for my parody selves, this story changes, but never in the right way. The differences never shed any new light, never lead to a satisfying place. The hurt still hurts as it will always hurt even as I try to change, hopelessly editing the story of my past until I'm contented with where I've been, who I am, changing as I try to change.

Yet this psychic wound remains. I cannot write this pain away.

–Portland, Maine
2006

III

(DREAMS)

I've my father's
taste and hurt
and my mother's
worries and mouth
  to give
  and give.

—Owls, "Anyone Can Have
    a Good Time"

PAIN, HOWEVER, DOES HAVE a tendency to take care of itself. Which is maybe just another way of saying: pain changes.

ONE LAST PHOTOGRAPH. A small black and white snapshot of my mother, taken sometime in the mid-1950s. In the photo—its scalloped edges worn thin and curling—she stands half-turned toward the camera in a pale swimsuit, wet hair in pigtails and bare toes digging in the sand. In the background, her out-of-focus little brother stomps either into or out of the breaking waves. My mother—who at most is ten years old in this picture, though likely closer to seven—is looking at the camera and wearing the same half-mischievous, half-dangerous grin I can recall punctuating certain rarefied moments throughout my life. It's a winning smile. As in, she's got you charmed. As in, she's got you beat.

I'd be remiss if I did not also mention that drooping from her right hand with a professional sort of nonchalance is a small black gun.

Now of course, the pistol has to be a toy. The pistol has to be a toy. But that does not change at all what I recognize in this picture of my mother. She's made up her mind to squish some kind of bug. Her feelings won't get hurt whatsoever in the squishing.

As much as I love this picture of my mother as a young girl, I am also acutely aware that it is indicative—or maybe the primary evidence of—a real challenge Mum presented to everyone who knew her. To a degree, my father was correct in his summation: there was a certain malice in her need to win in any given situation, irrespective of the stakes or their magnitude. During the prolonged and ugly suit for parental custody, Mum included in her testimony jabs at my father's penis-size and sexual behavior, details she knew were inadmissible and could possibly land her in contempt of court yet nevertheless felt compelled to air: they allowed her to cut my father down in a public theater. In a sense, her need to wound my father's dignity on the record superseded any maternal instinct (these antics, after all, couldn't possibly win her any points in the judge's purview). Compare that to her nuking any argument with me—any time I contradicted her, any time I refused to bend to her will—by insisting through gnashed teeth, *you are just like your father*. A man who attempted to strangle Mum with a telephone wire while I watched. A man who tried to push my sister down the cellar stairs. *You are just like your father*. When it came to getting what she wanted, the rate or depth of casualty simply did not matter.

So if the toy pistol in the photo had been real, would she have hesitated in shooting her little brother, the most obvious annoying bug begging for a squishing? Maybe. But if she had shot him, I'm sure she'd have treated it like a joke, blown the whole thing off. *I only shot him a little bit, jeez*. In that respect, she really was more interested in wounding than killing.

I wanted to hit him again.

But this is all speculation.

I wanted to take his head and pop it across the lawn.

As far as I know, Mum never put a bullet in her brother.

Though of course, you don't need a gun to draw blood. If in an argument and presented with an incontrovertible fact, something that shattered the logic of her position, Mum oftentimes would respond simply by blowing a raspberry in your face. Without a doubt, it's a childish response. But when employed enough times, over the course of a lifetime of confrontation, the meaning of the gesture begins to take on more cutting nuance, becomes a more distinct kind of dismissal, announcing without words that all your ideas and all your beliefs—the foundations upon which your ethos and identity rest—amount to little more than a wet farting sound blown through puckered lips. I really can't think of a more effective way of expressing to someone how unimportant their puny thoughts might be.

The woman in that picture is crippled.

The woman in that picture is me.

Okay. That's a lot of negativity wrapped up in a photograph of a little girl playing at the beach. Well-founded negativity, sure, but still: a lot. So why do I love this photograph? Why is it, in fact, the only picture of my mother I keep on display in my home, tucked into the frame of my bedroom mirror? Well. Because it's the face of my mother, the version of her I want to remember most, to remember best. Because that dangerously playful smile was beautiful. Because it's a picture of Mum actually happy (even if that happiness is woven with a meanness). Because even though I love seeing that look of genuine joy in my mother's face and try to keep it most present and vivid in my mind, it's not an expression I got to see a whole lot when Mum was still alive.

MUM'S DEATH WAS BOTH sudden and prolonged and needlessly stupid and was maybe the result of nearly half a century of untreated depression or an equally long two-pack-a-day habit. It was maybe also the result of being married to an asshole who didn't care about her wishes. (Who can say!) Late in September 2008, while doing her morning aerobics, Mum suffered in near tandem a burst aneurysm in her occipital lobe and a catastrophic stroke. (How do we know she was doing morning aerobics? Because she was found still clutching her five-pound weights, sprawled face down on the floor in front of the TV.) She lost control over her body. She fell and smacked her forehead on the brick skirt surrounding the woodstove. So count that as the third head trauma she all at once had to make sense of that dog-day morning.

Too often, I wonder what Mum saw in the moment when her brain turned against her. What did she hear? What did she feel?

Why do you want to know all this?

This singularly unique moment in her life.

What is it that you're looking for, Douglas?

What was it like when the lights flared out?

In many ways, this was the moment of her death. I want this to be the moment of her death. In the quiet solitude of the farm she loved. Perhaps comforted by her menagerie of cats. By the scent of garden soil dusted between the pine floorboards. By the north wind wracking through the eaves. I want this to be the moment of her death. But when her husband arrived home from work eight hours later, she was still gasping panicked, labored breaths, so he called an ambulance and had her rushed first to Houlton

Regional Hospital, then to Maine Medical Center in Portland, where the hospital—without consulting or informing a single member of our family—had her medevaced to Tufts Medical in Boston, whereupon after three weeks in a coma with tubes snaking into her arms and her brainpan and her urethra and her trachea, she was finally allowed to die. Weeks away from her sixty-first birthday. Four hundred miles from home in a city she absolutely loathed.

Mum had been a hospice nurse for twenty years. She was acutely aware of the ever-presence of death. She might have been a little romantic in her notions, but she didn't bullshit herself or anyone around her when it came to her own eventual dying. She told us—her husband, my brother, my sister, myself—that she wanted to die a natural death. No machines. No invasive surgeries. She told us all: she wanted to die at home. She told us this at every available opportunity.

One of the last times I saw Mum alive (I do not count her three-week ICU stasis as life), she repeated her wishes again. *I want to just lie down like a fox in tall grass and die.* For real. That's what I mean about romantic. *Like a fox in tall grass.* I told her I respected her wishes and agreed, it's an ideal way to go. I told her I would do everything in my power to make sure she got the right kind of end. I told her that without power of attorney, there were limits to what I could do. I could suggest. I could persist. Beyond that, my hands were tied. She said she knew that. She agreed: I was probably the only one in the family who wouldn't hesitate in helping her die. She said she'd consider making me her proxy.

Six months later:

A sterile ward in a faraway city.

A shunt draining the fluid collecting around her brain.

A machine doing all the breathing for her lungs that refused to breathe.

And in every single CT scan, a big blacked-out dead zone of inactivity where her brain had begun to necrotize.

I want to just lie down like a fox in tall grass.

I respected her wishes. I did everything within my means. I suggested. I persisted. Yet always furious, her husband was unhearing to everything but the sound of my voice: a hateful refrain against which he could lash out. (Sometimes it seemed he only kept her alive because I insisted we let her die.) Without power of attorney, there was nothing else I could do.

By the end of October, the doctors finally conceded: there was no likelihood of recovery for Mum. Her husband could no longer deny the reality of our new world. We arranged for the devices to be removed from her head and arms and lungs, arranged for the morphine in incremental doses. So many weeks in waiting: it only took a few hours to be done.

AFTER WRITING THAT LAST SECTION, I needed a little break. It's been eight years, and still, without warning, I can be blindsided by my grief. Lightning striking the same exact place. Over and over again. Yet sometimes Mum's death is just information—a weather update on the day's news—and I can talk about it without feeling affected at all, to the point where I sometimes think I didn't even like Mum that much. Her combative mien. *(I wanted to take his head and pop it across the yard.)* Her stubborn lack of forgiveness. *(I wanted to hit him again.)* I can sometimes convince myself that I do not miss my mom. Yet clearly my heart now and then needs to remind me: I'm wrong. A blatting raspberry blown in my face.

So my mother dies and my heart is broken so I write it down and then have to walk away from what I've written. I stand in the morning light streaming in through the sliding glass door and look out at the Japanese maple rupturing in red buds in the backyard. There are sparrows in the maple's limbs. The sparrows are fucking. I watch sparrows fuck for a while, then write my partner a text message.

> *Watching sparrows fucking in the maple. What they lack*
> *in duration, they make up for in frequency.*

How many times have I tried to write about my mother's death and the repercussions that have shuddered through my life since? How many half-filled journal pages? How many failed attempts?

I'm still watching the rapid-fire fornicators when my partner writes me back.

> *Stamina takes many forms.*

How many times can I tell the same story?
One more time. And the time after that, too.
There's always one more time.

THERE IS NEVER A DREAM, after all these years, where I am not aware that Mum has died. And I dream of her all the time. It doesn't even feel weird anymore, hanging out with Mum a couple times a week. I see my mother more now than I did when she was alive. I feel like we're finally getting better at this mother-son thing.

I cannot recall when I finally gave up reminding her that she's dead: for a while it seemed really important that she remember. Like maybe she'd forgotten she was supposed to be somewhere else. Like maybe she didn't belong anymore among the living. Sometimes I'd let her down easy, take her aside and break the news in a hush, and she'd get sad and hang her head, barely whisper, *I know.*

Other times, exasperated, I'd holler to her the news. To which she'd blow a raspberry in my face.

What more efficient way to tell me?

It doesn't matter if I'm dead.

Your puny thoughts don't matter.

NEVER DO I TELL HER: *lie down like a fox in tall grass.*

Never do I ask her for the power to let her die.

SOMETIMES IN MY DREAMS, Mum dies again. Seizes in another stroke. Constrained blood vessels once more bursting in her brain. But even in those dreams, she's still around. Doofing in the kitchen in her blown-out underpants. Cross-legged on the couch with a crossword in her lap. While I mourn her loss a second time around. While I try to make sense of this hollow in my heart. She spreads jam on some toast. She feeds catnip to a cat. A double ghost domestically haunting the house she loved so much.

In last night's dream, for the first time ever, she died again and stayed dead.

OBVIOUSLY, I KNOW THESE dreams are just dreams. My subconscious on its own, working through its knots (or as my friend Michael once put it: *your brain did a thing*). Now and then I play with the notion that it really is Mum's ghost I'm interacting with, that this is how she's chosen to spend her afterlife. Making herself at home in the cobwebs of my memory. Reminding me that death doesn't matter. But believing that would require believing in a whole bunch of other stuff (e.g.: an afterlife). So logic wins out. My brain is just doing a thing.

You can fantasize about things.

Makes you feel not so useless.

The motivation behind what my brain is doing while I sleep seems pretty obvious, too. Sometimes I want to hold onto Mum and everything I've lost since she died. Other times I wish I could be shut of her, let her die and stay dead. My argument with her is never not an argument with myself.

Because there is an inevitability in being someone's child, how so much of your identity is bound in that of your parents'. Just as how there's an inevitability in being someone's parent, seeing yourself reflected again and again in your child. You don't get to choose what of yourself gets echoed, what's irrevocably tangled together. You can't help that it's there. Your feelings on the matter won't make it go away.

Mum's stubbornness is something I still find myself struggling to forgive. (Too often, I find myself silently reliving our arguments, dredging up bilious ephemera to file as new evidence against her.) Her inability to forgive is hard for me to forgive. I'm aware of that irony. But awareness changes nothing. I want to release myself and her memory of this mulish psychic wound. I tell myself: *let it go.* And maybe for a few hours, I do. Maybe even a whole day. Then I go to sleep and dream of the farm. Mum with her crosswords or Mum with her cats. Arguing or not arguing. Speaking or not speaking. Toast in the kitchen. Pole beans in the garden. From an open door watching the wind have its way with the tall meadow grass beyond.

WHEN I WAS SEVENTEEN and meeting my father for the first time in eight years, we went for a long, tense walk on Popham Beach, where the Kennebec River empties fiercely into the bay. We walked the strand bordering the churning confluence. We threw a stick repeatedly for Bill's dog to fetch from the surf. On our return walk back up the beach, I saw in our tracks how Bill and I each walked with our right foot notably out-turned. Which is to say: our footprints in the sand were identical. I remember thinking how Bill had been hit by a truck when he was a kid. I remember thinking: *what's my excuse?*

Had I learned to mimic Bill's lopsided gait when I was still a toddler?

What else had he taught me that I do not remember, do not know enough to see?

And this bullshit goes both ways.

How much of who I am did my parents recognize in themselves?

How much of what they saw did they wish was never there?

Jesus, you are just like your father.

You know, you're a lot like your mother, too.

Snide and vindictive.

There was no listening.

A person can live with that for only so long.

So much of who we are belongs to someone else.

But what's it mean?

Why does it have to mean anything?

IN THE MIDST OF those three hospital weeks between when Mum had her stroke and when she was finally taken off life support and allowed, at last, to die, my grandmother Barbara also suffered a massive stroke, also fell into an irreversible coma. She died within a week of my mother, and this time, I was in the room with her when she died.

I was sitting at the foot of her bed in the hospital in Calais, Maine. My uncle Greg was sitting at her side. He might have been holding her hand. It doesn't matter. I remember, in the tense still and silence of her room, I was thinking about the chord progression of a Jason Molina song. The song was "Being in Love." I was mentally rehearsing the different accents and embellishments of each chord. I remember thinking, *I got this*. I remember how this thought was interrupted by my uncle saying, "She's not breathing anymore."

This was my father's mother. Who once testified against her son's competence in safely raising me. Who risked losing her own son in order to protect me. Breathing her last breath beside me while my mind was somewhere else.

Less often, I dream about my grandmother, too. She is also always dead in my dreams. As in, she's decaying. I never remind her that she's died.

The first time my uncle Greg and I met was in another hospital room, one not dissimilar to the room where Barbara would eventually die. He had flown out to Maine to visit his mother when, in the middle of his stay, she suffered some sort of pulmonary distress and had to undergo observation. What was meant to be a vacation suddenly became a weeks'-long sojourn, talking with doctors and orchestrating her care. When I got word of Barbara's hospitalization, I drove the four hours up to Calais from Portland to see her. It wasn't long after I arrived, sitting on the corner of my grandmother's bed, that Greg walked in the room. Even in her sickness, Barbara had to laugh. Here we were, two bearded strangers with flat cheeks and curly hair, each measuring the other up with skeptical, deeply-lined eyes while standing guard over this wounded woman central to their lives. It would have taken some hard accounting to disprove our resemblance. Even our posture was the same.

I know this seems like it's beyond the point of this long fractured essay about home and identity, but it's really not. In some ways, this *is* the point. My grandmother's slow and eventual death is what created the circumstances for me to have a relationship with my closest remaining paternal male relative. I have since spent months on his farm in the Central Valley, futzing with his landscaping and biking through the unending acreage of almond trees, wrestling with his wolf hounds and renaming his cats. He introduced me to my grandfather. He's the one who first told me about—and eventually took me to see—the California ghost towns that proved instrumental to the plot of my first novel.

And in the same way that I gained an uncle and grandfather in my grandmother's death, I also gained my cousins and aunt through Mum's death. Fearing I was alone and without family (not entirely true), they began involving themselves more in my life. Flying me out for holidays. Keeping me safe and fed when I otherwise might not have chosen to do so. In one particular instance, guiding me home through a Texas night while I was joyfully lost in a whiskey blackout.

These are family I would not have if I hadn't lost other parts of my family. They have taught me things. They have made me feel comfortable—if only for the duration of a phone call, of a glass of beer—in a world where I so often feel I do not belong. I know you cannot place a value on these sorts of things. But still, the mind explores the terrain it wants to, asks the questions that do not have answers. Was it worth the loss to gain what I gained? I can't know. Or maybe I just don't want to.

A FEW MONTHS AFTER our undocumented conversation in his February living room, Bill sent me a nondescript birthday card with a personal check enclosed. I had known this card would come. For most of my life, the compulsory birthday card comprised the near totality of our regular contact (I could usually count on a card around Christmastime, too). I had, in fact, been fearing its arrival. Now that the predicted card had come, I had to decide how best to respond. I came very close to returning the card, envelope unopened. But I had to guarantee Bill hadn't written anything other than his signature inside (he hadn't). After a few days' thought, I mailed back the voided check. In a brief letter, I explained that I could not accept this gift. I explained how our last meeting had plunged me into a black despair that lasted for weeks. I did not mention that during that bleak measure of days, all I could do was slouch under some blankets and listen to the same Neutral Milk Hotel record over and over again. I did not mention the tremendous strain this had put on my relationship with the woman I lived with, a college girlfriend who had moved to Maine with me despite her (now verified) reservations. But I did explain how I could not continue to punish myself by trying to make him into my idea of a father. Every interaction I had with him left me wounded, and those wounds were slow to heal. I explained to him: *I cannot do this anymore.* Until he could treat me with honesty and compassion, I could not have him in my life.

As of this writing, it's been ten years since I mailed that letter to my father. I have not heard from Bill since.

I know, for my own wellbeing, I made the correct choice. I made the only safe choice available. But I can't help but feel like I'm keeping some rotten family tradition alive. To actively estrange myself from the man who actively estranged himself from his mother, his brother, his sister, his son.

It's possible we understand each other better than I had thought.

WHY DO I SUSPECT that Bill likewise understands me? Because he never replied to my letter.

I didn't want to hurt you, so I let you go.

Either he understood how it feels to be disappointed by a parent, or he too felt wounded by our relationship, exhausted from having to constantly defend himself from my probing questions, the uninvited memory of my mother that I could not help but embody.

I didn't want to hurt you.

It's possible I was as poisonous to him as he was to me.

I let you go.

We each wanted something from the other. But clearly, that something would not be ours. So I guess ultimately Bill and I agreed.

I cannot do this anymore.

I let you go.

LOSSES AND GAINS.

I lose my father. But I never really had a father. I lose my father and try to find him then choose to lose what I've found.

I lose my mother. But she haunts me in my sleep. Sometimes she helps me and sometimes she hassles me. Blows a raspberry in my face. And then she dies again. So I lose and lose her again.

But in her death, I gain my aunt Kris and her husband Richard. I gain my cousins Caitlin and Lydia.

But still: I lose my mother.

I lose my grandmother and she decomposes in my sleep. But I gain my uncle Greg and his wife Janice. Who treat me like their weird not-quite-son. I gain my grandfather. Who wishes I weren't always so sad.

I have my brother Jaison. I keep him. Though we're both changed.

I keep my sister Tanya.

But I lose the farm.

Together, we lose the farm.

We keep each other.

We lose our home.

ALL OF JAISON'S HAIR fell out after Mum died. It didn't happen all at once. But it didn't take too long, either. Count that among the most obvious, outward changes that Jaison and Tanya and I underwent. We all drank substantially more. Jaison and I smoked ten million cigarettes. Jaison and Tanya smoked acres of pot. (The night that Mum was finally allowed to die, the three of us sat parked on the roof of the Tuft's garage, Jai and Tanya getting high up front while in the back, I downed a pint of Dewar's White, we as a unified team setting the tone and methodology of grief we'd pursue for the months to come.) Tanya gained weight while Jai and I lost it. Jai's girlfriend threatened to leave him. Mine had already left. For entire weeks that following winter, I would stay inside, only leaving the house for smokes and beer while watching movies on endless loops. Tarkovsky's *Stalker*. Gus Van Sant's *Last Days*. With only slight variations in our attack and means, Jaison and Tanya and I were withdrawing from the world. All of our relationships suffered.

All except our relationship to one another. In that first year after Mum died, the three of us drew closer together than we'd ever been before. Closer even than in those dark, violent days when Mum and Bill's marriage was furiously collapsing. The way I remember it feeling was like we were an animal litter left on its own to fend for itself. Which I guess is what we were. Orphans. Back to protecting back with a wary eye turned on everything that wasn't us. It seemed for entire weeks, Jaison and Tanya were the only people I talked to. Sometimes cooing one another asleep over the phone at 3 am. *(You can fantasize about things.)* Sometimes just explaining how the most simple, pedestrian details of our lives seemed so alien and surreal now, insurmountable. *(Makes you feel not so useless.)* We were protecting each other as best we could. We might have been wounded and shell-shocked and increasingly self-medicated, but we could at least seek some kind of solace in one another. We were going to survive this together. We held on to what little we had left.

IN TERMS OF THE MATERIAL, there was very little left to hold on to. Mum didn't have a will. Or if she did, it was homemade and too well-hidden. Or maybe found and strategically destroyed. Regardless. After her estate went through probate, Mum's widower essentially bought out my siblings' and my shares of the farm: we each got a few thousand dollars and little else. Tanya got Mum's jewelry. Jaison got Mum's record collection. I got a coffee cup. This was the sum of our inheritance. The physical evidence that our mother was ever real. (When Jaison and I arrived at the farm for what would prove to be our final time together to collect some of Mum's personal effects, her widower insisted he'd shoot us if we ever again stepped foot on his property, a threat we had no reason to doubt: quick as we could, we loaded up the few boxes her widower'd stacked haphazardly in the garage—mostly garbage, old nightgowns and underwear, stuff not even Goodwill could want—while he stood sentry at the front door like a foaming guard dog ready to snap. We weren't allowed inside the house. As far as he was concerned, we got more than we deserved.) Almost immediately following the estate's execution, Mum's widower remarried, then shortly thereafter died too. Thus, in a swift passage of months, our home—our mother's home—transferred in title and deed into the hands of her final husband's children and stepchildren and bride, into whatever unknowable motivations and intentions they might harbor. The farm and everything attached to it was gone.

It's hard not to feel angry about this. For Mum, the farm had never been just a piece of land. It was a concept. A parachute in case any of us fell. No matter how dire our lives proved to be, Jaison and Tanya and I would always have one safe place in the world. An outpost on the border designed for retreat. An isolated farm on a dead-end road.

You can fantasize about things.

Mum spent thirty-five years—almost her entire adult life—safeguarding this sanctuary for us. But she didn't complete the one protection that mattered. No notarized testament filed with the clerk's office. No legal document stating her will. Which meant her ideas and efforts meant nothing. No sanctuary. No refuge. Just a disputed property to be divided among three children and an increasingly destabilized widower. Her heir apparent with power of attorney. We lost everything because Mum married an asshole.

THERE IS A REASON why I've barely mentioned my mother's last husband. There is a reason why in this book he does not get a name. He does not deserve a name. If I knew of any possible way to complete this account without referring to his existence, you would never even know Mum had married a third and final time.

All I will say is this:

Of all the destructive things my father can be held responsible for in my and my family's lives, they are nothing compared to what his replacement found the time and imagination to execute. Two fucking decades of spite and venom. Endless threats. Endless hate. Finally ended. I cannot express how grateful I am to know without doubt that he's been removed permanently from our lives.

Though of course, as with every other ghost, I still have to deal with the asshole in my dreams. But he's harmless now. Emasculated in sleep. He can't hurt anyone anymore in my dreams.

He will not be mentioned again in this story.

TANYA RECENTLY TOLD ME over the phone that she was finally able to talk about Mum without breaking into tears. I laughed and said, "And to think, it only took the better part of a decade!" But I don't think she found it quite so funny as I did.

Meanwhile, I've spent the past three days drafting this conclusion with a continual tightness in my throat and an ache behind my eyes, never quite knowing if these tears will ever come.

Stamina takes many forms.

Perhaps I cannot afford to be so callously flip.

These past few years, I've convinced myself that I've moved past all these tumultuous things I've come to associate with home. But as I attempt to finally write it all down, it's clear I haven't yet escaped from under that black cloud. I know: what I'm feeling now is not the same as what I felt ten years ago. Twenty years ago. Thirty years ago. The pain changes. But it never goes away. Never better and never worse. Only different, always new.

The things my father has said and done still hurt me. The way a bum knee aches in wet weather. It's manageable.

Would that boy be any less you than you are?

Usually.

It doesn't define me.

Any less you.

Just as Mum's choices—to never apologize, to never forgive—continue to hurt me.

Jesus, you are just like your father.

Like a cracked tooth you can't afford to fix or have pulled. Most of the time, it's okay. But sometimes, it's unbearable.

BUT WHAT, EXACTLY, DOES *lost* in this context even mean? Is it to have an allotment of your life and world erased from the atlas of your identity? Or does it simply mean that what was yours is now another's? Or, simpler yet, what was yours is now not yours. Nothing is gone. Nothing is erased. You just can't call it your home anymore.

Why do you keep coming here?

What is it that you're looking for, Douglas?

In April 2015, I accepted an invitation to give a reading at the Maine School of Science and Mathematics, the residential magnet school where I completed my last two years of high school. The last time I'd driven north into Aroostook County was October 2009, when Jaison and I made our doomed attempt to save any tangible evidence that our mother had existed. In the six intervening years since our violent banishment from the farm, I'd convinced myself that I did not miss this remote stretch of America's end. (After all, why pine after what you can never have back?) The invitation all at once had me doubting that conviction.

My partner, Genevieve—the woman with whom I now live—wanted to join me on this trip, wanted to see where I was raised and witness with her own eyes this strange place few people have ever been, see the locations that, in my stories' retellings, had taken on legendary proportions. The hoarder at the top of Drake's Hill who'd turned his entire property into a cramped junk-sculpture park. The famous dairy bar whose ice cream I've witnessed convert devout vegans. The sweeping potato deserts. The shoulder-rolling terrain. And I wanted to show her. I was eager to. Which meant maybe I'd missed the place after all.

The day before we left, I called the town manager's office. I had heard various rumors as to how the farm had changed hands more than once since Mum's death, but I had no idea who owned the place now. I wanted Genevieve to see the house, the land, the western horizon etched indelibly in my memory. I wanted to see it for myself. But I had to make sure it was safe. I had to know who owned the farm.

"The old customhouse?" the woman on the other end of the line asked.

At that, I had to laugh. It'd been at least forty years since the brick house down the road from our farm had been used for any kind of official border activity. Yet still: "the old customhouse." It was reassuring to know how long the memory of the landscape persists.

"Two houses further down the way," I told her. "The last house on Lincoln Road."

"Okay. Hold on one second."

I could hear her open a cabinet drawer—that unmistakable rumble and squeak—could hear fingers moving among the records. I was amazed at how easy this process was proving to be: ask a question, get an answer.

"Yep. It's the Amish."

"The Amish?"

"Mm-hmm. They been buying up lots of farms out that way."

"Oh."

The Amish.

I imagined black hats with buckles on the bands. I pictured beards without mustaches.

The woman on the phone asked if I needed anything else. I remember, she called me *dear*. I told her no, thank you, that just about does it. She wished me a good day. We hung up.

The Amish.

No shit.

I had called the town office to learn if the farm was safe.

The Amish sounded pretty safe.

WHEN WE WERE KIDS, Jai and I both often dreamed about the farm. The long rolling hills painted in the near-black of evergreens, the bone-white of poplars and the tawny blonde fields. The far-off ghosts of the Appalachians bluely haunting the horizon. In our dreams, the farm was always the site of a battle or some other impending disaster inexorably closing in. An army of undead. A virus or pestilential worm. A tidal wave crushing impossibly up the hills. Mum, I remember, would have these dreams, too. Always in the dreams, we were on the losing side of the war.

When I dream of the farm now, things are quiet. There are cats and rabbits in the grass outside. Jaison naps on a living room couch. Mum is dead or has just died again and is making a pie in the kitchen. This is what passes for normal these days. The crisis we waited all our lives for has come and gone. We lost. In its aftermath, finally, we can relax.

I have no idea what my brother dreams about anymore.

THERE WAS STILL SNOW on the ground in Aroostook County that April. But the air was warm when the breeze was still. What of the Earth we could see just seemed an excuse to justify the stunning vault of sky.

Genevieve and I stayed at a motel. We swam in the pool and had drinks in the lounge. We ate dinner at a place called Burger Boy. Wherever we went, people always wanted to talk to us. Complete strangers. This was really startling to me. Growing up here, I'd never considered folks to be friendly. Then again, I had been a blatantly weird kid, as likely to quote Paramahansa Yogananda as I was Maynard James Keenan, leering wolfish with hair twisting down to the belt of my black Navy-issue trench coat. It's possible I'd been the one who was unfriendly.

In the morning, we drove over to my old school. I met some of the students. I met with old friends who were now teachers and administrators. I gave a reading and signed some books. I had an overwhelmingly positive time.

Then Genevieve and I drove south to my hometown.

We stood in the market square and watched the Meduxnekeag River drift slowly behind the buildings.

We walked around the library where I had once spent entire summer days.

We got an ice cream at the famous dairy bar.

We did a slow drive-by of the hoarder's palisade of handmade lawn art.

We started toward the farm.

Fields snow-swept and deep brown with wet. Fields shaggy with dried winter rye. Silos and spotted cows. Farmhouses wherein I might still know people's names.

Why do you keep coming here?

What is it that you're looking for, Douglas?

"This," I said as I turned the car onto Lincoln Road, "is starting to feel like something."

Like a fox in tall grass.

Beside me, Genevieve took my hand. She stroked my hair and massaged the muscle between my forefinger and thumb. Slowly, I let out a long breath, my head light and swimmy. I may or may not have eaten a Klonopin at the dairy bar.

Throughout our trip north, a handful of CDs had been on steady rotation. A mix of underground hip-hop. Busdriver's *Beaus$Eros*. Both albums by Owls. So while it feels like an artful construction to say so, it is plausible—and, in fact, I am almost certain—that on the stereo, Owls were playing "Anyone Can Have a Good Time."

> *We lose each other.*
> *We've no right not to.*

Regardless. Passing the first farms of Lincoln Road, I punched the stereo off.

Changes were evident before we crested the first hill. It appeared the woman on the phone had been right: the Amish had bought up a lot of the land on Lincoln Road. A dairy farm. A potato farm. A wood lot. Fallow fields. All being worked now by ascetic Christians.

"Holy shit," I said. "Things are *happening* up here."

Gasping, Genevieve pointed at a tall black horse standing by a house in the field. The horse was new. The house was new, too.

"That thing's huge," she said. "It's taller than a person."

Which was true. A man was standing alongside the horse, running a curry brush over its flank. His head barely reached its shiny black shoulder.

"I used to get high in that field," I told her. But that was non-information. I got high in all these fields.

Rounding the bend just past what I grew up thinking of as Leroy Crane's farm, we approached the old brick customhouse—ascending the hill, the road now paralleling the Canadian border—and in the field behind the house, silhouetted against the sky: a man in a tall hat driving a pair of horses pulling a tiller. Great clods of dirt flew high up in their wake. Like a schooner making waves, ripping through the earth.

Cruising by, we watched the flying dirt in awestruck stupefaction. It did not seem possible this was real.

We passed the brick customhouse and a field half-ribbed in snow. We passed the blackened cellar hole where our nearest neighbor's shanty once stood. The farm came into view.

"Baby," Genevieve breathed. "There's a windmill."

"Yeah. That's Mum's windmill."

I guess I'd forgotten to tell her there was a windmill.

"How are you feeling?" she asked, again stroking my hair.

Like a fox in tall grass.

In a *shooshing* outrush of held air: "I'm feeling."

We've no right not to.

We passed the last field and pulled to a stop at the rutted driveway's end.

The sagging garage.

The clouded breezeway window.

The original farmhouse, over a hundred and fifty years old, clapboards weathered grey.

The addition and greenhouse out back where the barn and ell used to stand.

The sloping backyard crusted in old snow.

The dormant raspberry patch and line of apple trees.

The wrecked tumble of the chicken house.

The rolling shoulders of the hills.

The indelible western horizon.

What is it that you're looking for, Douglas?

We got out of the car and approached the house.

Why do you keep coming here?

I never thought I'd be this kind of person.

We introduced ourselves to the people inside.

ONE OF MY EARLIEST MEMORIES is of the yard behind the house, between my sandbox and the nasty slouch of the old chicken house. I'm toddling downhill which means toddling west. I see a black and white bumble bee wrestling with itself in the grass. Identifying the bee as something that stings, I decide to neutralize the threat. I step on the black and white bee. When I lift my foot, the bee flies up to sting my meaty left arm.

So much for mitigating danger.

But I'm stalling again. I'm stalling because I'm afraid. I'm not ready yet for this story to end. Once it's over, what more will I be able to say? What choice will I have but to finally let it go? Let go of the home I cannot have. Let go of my family and what we used to be. Everything that hurt and all that I loved.

I didn't want to hurt you, so I let you go.

This time, I don't want to have the last word.

So much for mitigating pain.

JAKE AND SAVILLA ARE originally from Missouri. It was only a few years ago that they took a train and then a bus from their longtime home to join the Amish community in Smyrna, Maine. When the community opted to start a satellite colony and bought up the lion's share of Lincoln Road, Jake and Savilla moved into Mum's farm.

"We've only been here since January," Savilla tells us. "We're still getting to know the place."

A neatly tied bonnet.

A beard without a mustache.

Jake and Savilla are in their sixties. They quite happily invite Genevieve and me inside the house. Their home. They invite us inside their home. We sit at their kitchen table and eat molasses cookies, drink sweet apple cider preserved in a mason jar. It's warm with the woodstove's roar. Add a cloud of cigarette smoke and a massive kola bud drying from the bay-window pane and this could be a perfect reenactment of a scene from thirty years ago.

Outside, Jake and Savilla's corgi sniffs around in the crusty snow. In the garage, their little dark horse snorts and stamps its hay.

Honestly, I'm not sure what I was expecting would happen, visiting this place again. Maybe we'd just look at the house from outside. Confirm that it still exists or maybe no longer exists. I don't think I expected to be welcomed inside, to sit talking for two hours in my former kitchen. I don't think I expected to answer so many questions.

"Why is the floor in one half of the root cellar a full foot higher than the other half?"

"Why does the greenhouse have so little glass?"

"What is this thing in the bathroom?"

For my part, I answer as best I can.

"I guess they got tired of digging that part.

"I don't think Mum knew how a greenhouse was supposed to be.

"That's a whirlpool."

"A whirlpool?" Savilla asks.

"It's like a fancy bathtub."

Jake nods. "I use it to fill the bucket when I water the horse."

"Yeah, and track mud through the house when you do it, too."

"I can show you where there's an outside spigot."

They consider this a good turn of fortune. They had not known there was a spigot outside. This place that still feels so familiar to me, so present in my memory, is a mystery to these new inheritors.

Jake wants to know about the line of apple trees out back. Savilla wants to know what other plantings are about. I can tell Genevieve's curious about these things as well. Eventually, we all go outside.

"Now what is this thing supposed to be?" Savilla asks me. She's bent to pick up some Styrofoam thing off the ground by the back deck.

"That's just some trash," I say. The last residents left trash everywhere. Filthy throw rugs and plastic nothings half-buried in the snow. "Just some trash someone left behind."

Jake and Savilla seem less affected by this news than I am: why would someone choose to strew garbage over their own lawn? Why with intention make shitty something so nice?

Would that boy be any less you?

Above the hills, the western sky is turning pink. Spruce and fir near-black against the snow. Bone-white poplars. Tawny dead-grass fields.

Why do you keep coming here?

The windmill's frozen blades.

What is it that you're looking for, Douglas?

The stump where my brother Daniel's memorial tree was chopped down.

Stamina takes many forms.

I show Jake and Savilla and Genevieve where the chives and catnip and borage will soon sprout from the thawing ground. The rose bush and lilac and magnolia I planted for Mum in the summer of 2006. The unstrung clothesline, just two wooden crosses set several yards apart. The tire swing, still snowbound, descending from the crown of the front yard's sugar maple. The landmarks that once defined my home.

While I talk to Jake and Savilla, Genevieve crouches to ruffle the corgi's orange fur. A cool wind blows in from the north. That ruffles the dog's fur too.

"You're telling me that's a magnolia?" Jake says. We're standing at the rock retaining wall my brother and I helped build—a long tapered gore of slate terracing the driveway above the sloping backyard—looking south toward the winter-nude tree. "This far north?"

"Yep. It's the hardiest variety, as far as I know. A Dr. Merrill magnolia. *Magnolia x loebneri.*" The tips of its branches each uprise in a fuzzy grey bud. Like a pussy willow or a rabbit's foot. "It's looking good. It should bloom like crazy for you guys soon."

It will take a few weeks to process this moment before I understand what I'm feeling. But it's relief. I'm feeling the giddy sweetness of relief. Relief to have this last surprise chance to see my former home. Relief to discover these people now watching over the farm. This place is no longer mine. But it's safe. In this moment, that's what matters most. This home is finally safe. Mum had wanted so much for this place to be a refuge removed from the rest of the world. A piece of fertile earth to be worked. A life sustained by the land. She could never quite make that happen for herself. But these people can.

"Where would be a good place to plant a garden?" Jake asks me, and with the southern fields unfolding below us toward the far-off pines, I cannot help but smile. I'd planted the magnolia at the northwest corner of Mum's vegetable garden. I didn't want it to out-shade the tender things she grew.

"Right here," is what I tell him. "You're looking at it."

—Scarborough, Maine
2016

Douglas W. Milliken is a queer composer, artist, and writer based in Saco, Maine.

Fomite

Writing a review on social media sites for readers will help the progress of independent publishing. To submit a review, go to the book page on any of the sites and follow the links for reviews. Books from independent presses rely on reader-to-reader communications.

For more information or to order any of our books, visit:
http://www.fomitepress.com/our-books.html

More Odd Birds from Fomite...

William Benton
Eye La View

Michael Breiner
the way none of this happened

Roger Coleman
The World Was Late

Bill Davis
Cheap Gestures

Clare Dolan
Museum of Everyday Life

J. C. Ellefson
Under the Influence: Shouting Out to Walt

Stephen J. Goldberg
Rants Raves & Ricochets

Joel Grossman
Reading Embodied

Fomite

David Ross Gunn
Cautionary Chronicles

Andrei Guriuanu &Teknari
Portraits of Time
The Darkest City

Gail Holst-Warhaft
The Fall of Athens

Sam Kerson
Executions and Democracy
Gaza Punishing the Innocent

Michael Jewell
The Memoirs of a Paper Doll

Daniil Kharms
Connections (translator Roger Lebovitz, artist Delia Robinson)

Roger Lebovitz
A Guide to the Western Slopes and the Outlying Area
Obscure Blessings
Twenty-two Instructions for Near Survival

Pippo Lionni
Fat Facts of Life

dug Nap
Artsy Fartsy
Friends

Fletcher Oakes
Modern Mandalas

Fomite

Puppeteers
  Sourdough Rising

Delia Bell Robinson
  A Shirtwaist Story
  The Waters Prevail

Claire Russell
  Dear Mr. Thoreau

Clark Russrll
  Riddleville

Peter Schumann
  A Child's Deprimer
  Abrakadabra Yes No Apocalypse
  All
  All, Nothing, Nothing at All
  Bedsheet Mitigations
  PBelligerent & Not So Belligerent Slogans from the Possibilitarian Arsenal
  Bread & Sentences
  Declaration of Light/Quo Vadis
  Diagonal Man Theory + Praxis, Volumes One and Two
  Erbarme dich – Have Mercy
  Es is vollbracht - Mission Accomplished
  Faust 3
  Gaza Genocide Bedsheets
  Handouts and Obligations
  Kropotkin Speaks
  Life and Death of Charlotte Salomon
  Mister Aeschylus's The Persians
  Planet Kasper, Volumes One and Two

Fomite

www.ingramcontent.com/pod-product-compliance
Lightning Source LLC
Chambersburg PA
CBHW081536120626
46550CB00009B/2749

* 9 7 8 1 9 5 9 9 9 8 4 2 4 5 *